T0266350

www.ingramcontent.com/pod-product-compliance
Lightning Source LLC
Jackson TN
JSHW052138131224
75386JS00039B/1297

9 780867 050585

The
TIME FOR PRAYER
Program

זְמַן לִתְפִילָה

BOOK 2: שְׁמַע
Dina Maiben and Hillary Zana

Project Consultant and Hebrew Advisor: Rivka Dori

Editors: Raymond A. Zwerin
 Audrey Friedman Marcus

Illustrations: Hal Aqua

Published by:
A.R.E. Publishing
An Imprint of Behrman House, Inc.
Millburn, New Jersey
www.behrmanhouse.com

© A.R.E. Publishing, Inc. 1998

ISBN-10: 0-86705-058-6
ISBN-13: 978-0-86705-058-5

Printed in the United States of America

Dear Students,

בְּרוּכִים הַבָּאִים!

Welcome to the second book in the זְמַן לִתְפִילָה program. By now, you've had the chance to sharpen your reading skills, review some Hebrew words, and learn some important blessings. In this book you will:

- continue to practice your reading skills
- begin to study the prayers in the service
- learn how to pray
- discuss some important ideas about God and prayer
- explore some key Hebrew prayer words
- add to your treasury of Hebrew words.

The major prayer in this book is the שְׁמַע, which you may already know well. Now you will study the prayers that come before and after it. This part of the service is like a journey. So grab your packs, fill your canteens, and get ready to explore the שְׁמַע and its blessings!

Pack Up Your Reading Skills

Practice reading these words.

1.	שַׁבָּת	אַבָּא	אִשָּׁה	דָּג	שֶׁמֶשׁ	הָאִמָּא	הַגָּדָה	מַגִּיד	אַתָּה
2.	שָׁנָה	אֲנִי	בְּיָד	הוּא	הִיא	אָדָם	דָּגָן	קָדוֹשׁ	צִיצִית
3.	לָבָן	חוּמְצָה	מִצְוָה	שַׁלְוָה	אָבִיב	רָחוּם	בַּקְבּוּק	הַבְדָּלָה	הַתִּקְוָה
4.	הָרַע	אֱמֶת	נֶאֱמָן	עֶרֶב	יִשְׂרָאֵל	עָלֵינוּ	חַיֵּינוּ	אָבִינוּ	מַלְכֵּנוּ
5.	סוֹף	חֹרֶף	מַעֲשֶׂה	אֹפֶן	מְזוּזָה	מְזוֹנוֹת	טֹטָפוֹת	אֲבוֹתֵינוּ	לְהִתְעַטֵּף
6.	יִשַׁי	אָזִי	לְעוֹלָם	מֵאֶרֶץ	בְּחֻקֶּיךָ	הַפּוֹרֵשׁ	יִתְבָּרַךְ	מַעֲשֶׂיךָ	מִצְוֹתַי

CHAPTER **1**
"The 99 Million Names of God"

דַף קְרִיאָה
READING PAGE

FOCUS ON PHONICS: חַ ָ

KEY WORDS YOU SHOULD KNOW

חַג שָׂמֵחַ

לְבָנֶיךָ	אֱלֹהֵנוּ	וַאֲנַחְנוּ	עָלֵינוּ	וְהָאָרֶץ	מֶלֶךְ .1
פּוֹרֵחַ	סוֹלֵחַ	אוֹרֵחַ	תַּפּוּחַ	לוּחַ	רוּחַ .2
בְּהַצְלָחָה	מַצְלִיחַ	מַבְטִיחַ	שָׁלִיחַ	מָלוּחַ	רֵיחַ .3
הַמִּזְבֵּחַ	לְשַׁבֵּחַ	בּוֹקֵעַ	לִקְבּוֹעַ	נְזַבֵּחַ	שָׂמֵחַ .4
מִזְרָח	לִזְרוֹחַ	זוֹרֵחַ	וַיִּזְרַח	שֶׁבַח	כֹּחַ .5
מַקְדֵּחָה	מְתֻנְבֵּחַ	וְכֹחַ	פְּתוּחָה	פּוֹתֵחַ	שָׂמַח .6

Most often, Hebrew words are stressed on the last syllable. When the stress falls on a different syllable, this mark is used: ▌ *as in* אֱלֹהֵנוּ. *Practice being a Super Reader. Read these phrases smoothly with the stress on the correct syllables.*

1. מָעוֹז + צוּר + יְשׁוּעָתִי =   מָעוֹז צוּר יְשׁוּעָתִי

2. לְךָ + נָאֶה + לְשַׁבֵּחַ =   לְךָ נָאֶה לְשַׁבֵּחַ

3. תִּכּוֹן + בֵּית + תְּפִלָּתִי =   תִּכּוֹן בֵּית תְּפִלָּתִי

4. וְשָׁם + תּוֹדָה + נְזַבֵּחַ =   וְשָׁם תּוֹדָה נְזַבֵּחַ

5. לְעֵת + תָּכִין + מַטְבֵּחַ =   לְעֵת תָּכִין מַטְבֵּחַ

6. מִצָּר + הַמְנַבֵּחַ =   מִצָּר הַמְנַבֵּחַ

7. אָז + אֶגְמוֹר + בְּשִׁיר + מִזְמוֹר =   אָז אֶגְמוֹר בְּשִׁיר מִזְמוֹר

8. חֲנֻכַּת + הַמִּזְבֵּחַ =   חֲנֻכַּת הַמִּזְבֵּחַ.

These phrases are taken from a prayer that is very popular at Chanukah time. It describes God as being a "Mighty Fortress" Who is worthy of our highest praise, and it reminds us that the Maccabees rededicated the Temple in Jerusalem.

Rhymes & Reasons

Does each pair of words rhyme or not? Circle the letter in the correct answer column. Then fill the letter answers into the blanks below to learn about the Key Word, שֵׁם.

DOES NOT RHYME	RHYMES		
ס	(ט)	הָפוּךְ	נָמוּךְ	1.
ו	ו	אֱלֹהֵנוּ	אַהֲלוּ	2.
ב	ף	שֶׁלְּךָ	שָׁלַק	3.
שָׁ	שֶׁ	יִשְׁלַח	שֶׁלְּךָ	4.
ם	שׁ	נִפּוּק	נָפוּחַ	5.
מְ	ט	בַּדֶּרֶךְ	בָּרוּךְ	6.
שֶׁ	כָּ	פּוּךְ	תַּפּוּחַ	7.
מַ	צַ	כֹּחַ	כֹּה	8.
ו	ז	לְבָבֶךָ	בְּבֵיתֶךָ	9.
ד	ט	אָח	פֵּךְ	10.
ג	ו	פְּתוּחָה	מְנוּחָה	11.
ב	ו	אֶשְׁכָּחֵךְ	שׁוֹלֵחַ	12.

ט

___ ___ ___ ___ ___ ___ ___ ___ ___ ___ ___ ___
12 11 10 9   8   7   6   5   4   3   2   1

"A good name is more precious than fine oil."
(Ecclesiastes 7:1)

טוֹב שֵׁם מִשֶּׁמֶן טוֹב
(קֹהֶלֶת ז׳ א׳)

What is your שֵׁם? _____

The 99 Million Names of God

1. הַשֵׁם — The Name
2. יְיָ / אֲדֹנָי — The Eternal One, or Adonai
3. י-ה-ו-ה — The Eternal One, or Adonai
4. אֱלֹהִים — God
5. אֱלֹהֵינוּ — Our God
6. מֶלֶךְ הָעוֹלָם — Ruler of the World or Universe
7. שׁוֹכֵן עַד מָרוֹם — The One Who Inhabits Eternity
8. מֶלֶךְ מַלְכֵי הַמְּלָכִים — The Ruler of All the Rulers
9. אָבִינוּ מַלְכֵּנוּ — Our Parent, Our Ruler
10. אֲדוֹן עוֹלָם — Ruler of Time and Space
11. הָרַחֲמָן — The Compassionate One
12. הַקָדוֹשׁ בָּרוּךְ הוּא — The Sacred and Blessed One
13. מֶלֶךְ מוֹחֵל וְסוֹלֵחַ — The Forgiving Ruler
14. אֵין סוֹף — The One Without End
15. אַב הָרַחֲמִים — Source of Compassion
16. אֵל שַׁדַּי — God the Almighty
17. רִבּוֹנוֹ שֶׁל עוֹלָם — Sovereign of the Universe
18. שׁוֹמֵר יִשְׂרָאֵל — Guardian of Israel
19. צַדִּיק הָעוֹלָמִים — The Just One of All Worlds
20. בּוֹרֵא עוֹלָם — Creator of the Universe
21. יְדִיד נֶפֶשׁ — Beloved of My Soul
22. קְדוֹשׁ יִשְׂרָאֵל — The Sacred One of Israel
23. שְׁכִינָה — God's Presence
24. הַמָּקוֹם — The Place
25. דַּיָן הָאֱמֶת — The True Judge
26. יְיָ צְבָאוֹת — Adonai of Hosts (Army of Angels)
27. הַמָּקוֹר — The Source
28. עוֹשֶׂה מַעֲשֵׂה בְרֵאשִׁית — Maker of the Wonders of Creation

(Moses asks God)

"When I go to the Children of Israel and tell them the God of their ancestors has sent me, and they ask me Your Name, what shall I tell them?"

(God answers)

"I AM THAT I AM. Tell the Children of Israel that 'I AM' has sent you."

Based on Exodus 3:13–14
שמות ג' י"ג - י"ד

KEY WORD: שֵׁם

In our tradition, people have used many names to describe God. A midrash teaches: "God said, 'My name is according to My work. When I judge, my Name is אֱלֹהִים (God). When I make war on the wicked, it is צְבָאוֹת (Hosts). When I withhold judgment, it is שַׁדַּי (Almighty). When I show compassion, it is אֲדֹנָי (Adonai).'" — *Exodus Rabba* 3.6

With a partner, read the list of God's names on page 6 and answer the questions.

1. Find a name that describes a God who:

   cares_____   creates_____

   is powerful_____   is just_____

   forgives_____   is infinite_____

   None of the above _____

2. Why do you think we use so many different names for God?

   _____

The prayer on the next page uses four different names for God in each verse.

CHAPTER **1**

אֵין כֵּאלֹהֵינוּ

There is none like our God;	אֵין כַּאדוֹנֵינוּ	1. אֵין כֵּאלֹהֵינוּ
there is none like our Eternal;	אֵין כְּמוֹשִׁיעֵנוּ.	2. אֵין כְּמַלְכֵּנוּ
there is none like our Ruler;		
there is none like our Rescuer.	מִי כַאדוֹנֵינוּ	3. מִי כֵאלֹהֵינוּ
Who is like our God? Our Eternal?	מִי כְמוֹשִׁיעֵנוּ.	4. מִי כְמַלְכֵּנוּ
Our Ruler? Our Rescuer?		
Give thanks to our God;	נוֹדֶה לַאדוֹנֵינוּ	5. נוֹדֶה לֵאלֹהֵינוּ
to our Eternal; to our Ruler;	נוֹדֶה לְמוֹשִׁיעֵנוּ.	6. נוֹדֶה לְמַלְכֵּנוּ
to our Rescuer.		
Blessed is our God; our Eternal;	בָּרוּךְ אֲדוֹנֵינוּ	7. בָּרוּךְ אֱלֹהֵינוּ
our Ruler; our Rescuer.	בָּרוּךְ מוֹשִׁיעֵנוּ.	8. בָּרוּךְ מַלְכֵּנוּ
You are our God; our Eternal;	אַתָּה הוּא אֲדוֹנֵינוּ	9. אַתָּה הוּא אֱלֹהֵינוּ
our Ruler; our Rescuer.	אַתָּה הוּא מוֹשִׁיעֵנוּ.	10. אַתָּה הוּא מַלְכֵּנוּ

The אֵין כֵּאלֹהֵינוּ prayer is an acrostic poem. In this special Hebrew poetic form the first letter of each verse spells out a hidden message. Crack the code. Complete the puzzle using the correct words from the word box. Write the letters from the shaded boxes onto the lines under the word box.

WORD BOX

אוֹר	יַיִן
שַׁבָּת	בַּר-מִצְוָה
בַּת-מִצְוָה	רֹאשׁ הַשָּׁנָה

1. What you see at the end of the night.
2. What you become at the end of childhood.
3. We drink this at the end of הַבְדָּלָה.
4. הַבְדָּלָה comes at the end of _____.
5. Not the end of the year, but its "head".

___ ___ ___ ___ ___
   ָ   ֵ   ָ

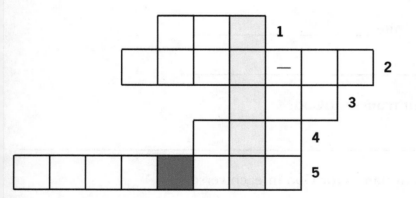

Rashi tells us that this spells אָמֵן בָּרוּךְ אַתָּה. By saying the end of a blessing (אָמֵן) followed by its two opening words (בָּרוּךְ אַתָּה) we are reminded that our praises for God should never end.

Who is he?   ?מִי הוּא

It's Mrs. Shapiro's first day of Hebrew school. Help her identify the students.
Fill in the blanks with הוּא, הִיא, or the right name.

הוּא _____

הִיא _____

_____ יוֹסִי

_____ רִבְקָה

_____ מִיכָאֵל

Turn back to page 8 and underline all the Hebrew pronouns in the prayer phrases.

What's in a Name?

Mrs. Shapiro's class was quietly completing their Hebrew pronoun worksheets. While she was answering questions, Yossi began writing on the board. When the board was covered, he shouted, "Mrs. Shapiro! Maybe this will answer their questions!" He read:

Mrs. Shapiro sighed. "Yossi, the year has only started and already you're making quite a name for yourself."

"What do you mean? My name's always been Yossi. See, it says so right on the board." The class giggled.

"Making a name for yourself means earning a reputation. When people hear the name Yossi, what do you want them to think?"

Esther called out, "Our public school teacher says his middle name is 'Trouble.' Is that what you mean, Mrs. Shapiro?"

Michael added, "Yossi is a nickname for Yosef. That's a name from the Torah."

"I can see we need to talk about this," Mrs. Shapiro said as she erased the board. "When people hear your name, they don't think about what it actually means or where it comes from. They think of your reputation, what kind of a person you are and how you act. In our tradition, having a good name is more important than money. In fact, it's the most important thing a person can have." Mrs. Shapiro picked up the chalk and wrote:

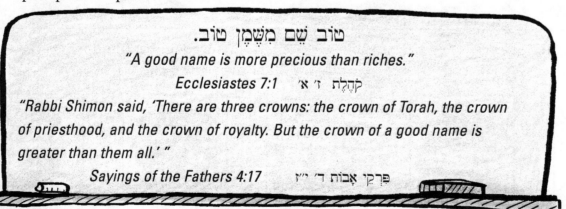

טוֹב שֵׁם מִשֶּׁמֶן טוֹב.
"A good name is more precious than riches."
Ecclesiastes 7:1   קֹהֶלֶת ז׳ א׳
"Rabbi Shimon said, 'There are three crowns: the crown of Torah, the crown of priesthood, and the crown of royalty. But the crown of a good name is greater than them all.' "
Sayings of the Fathers 4:17   פִּרְקֵי אָבוֹת ד׳ י״ז

"For homework, Yossi, I'd like you to list all the good things about yourself that you'd like people to remember when they hear your name. And be sure to include your 'sense of humor!'"

כֶּתֶר שֵׁם טוֹב

Help Yossi finish his homework by creating your own "Crown of a Good Name."

List some of the good qualities that people should know you have.

1. _____

2. _____

3. _____

"Everyone has three names: one your father and mother give you,
one that others call you, and one you acquire for yourself."

(Ecclesiastes Rabbah 7.1.3)

Language Enrichment

אוֹצַר מִלִּים
A TREASURY OF WORDS

Rebecca Mizrachi

Rebecca = שֵׁם פְּרָטִי

Mizrachi = שֵׁם מִשְׁפָּחָה

שֵׁם עִבְרִי = רִבְקָה

Becky = שֵׁם חִיבָּה

Daniel Cohen

Daniel = שֵׁם פְּרָטִי

Cohen = שֵׁם מִשְׁפָּחָה

שֵׁם עִבְרִי = דָּנִיאֵל

Danny = שֵׁם חִיבָּה

Fill in your three names in Hebrew or English.

1. _____ _____
שֵׁם מִשְׁפָּחָה   שֵׁם פְּרָטִי

2. _____
שֵׁם חִיבָּה

3. _____
כֶּתֶר שֵׁם טוֹב

"Of" or "Belonging to" = שֶׁל

"My" or "Mine" = שֶׁל + אֲנִי = שֶׁלִי

Help the customers get their dinners.
Read the story, then draw a line from each item to the correct placemat.

הַשֵּׁם שֶׁל הַיַּלְדָּה אֶסְתֵּר. הַשֵּׁם שֶׁל הַיֶּלֶד דָּנִיאֵל.

דָּנִיאֵל וְאֶסְתֵּר בְּבֵית-קָפֶה. אִמָּא שֶׁל אֶסְתֵּר בְּבֵית-קָפֶה.

דָּנִיאֵל: הַפִּיצָה שֶׁלִי.

אֶסְתֵּר: הַסְפָּגֶטִי וְהַמִילְק שֵׁיק שֶׁלִי.

דָּנִיאֵל: הַקּוֹלָה שֶׁלִי.

אִמָּא שֶׁל אֶסְתֵּר: הַתֵּה וְהַסָּלָט שֶׁלִי . . . אֲנִי בְּדִיאֶטָה.

KEY WORD:
עוֹלָם

דַּף קְרִיאָה
READING PAGE

KEY WORDS YOU SHOULD KNOW

מֹשֶׁה

all or every = כָּל

FOCUS ON PHONICS:

וּשׁ = שׁ ◻ שׁוֹ = שׁ ◻ = וּ = ◻ָ

וּבְכָל	וְכָל	לְכָל	מִכָּל	כָּל	הַכֹּל	1.
אָזְנַיִם	עֵינַיִם	חָפְשִׁי	חָכְמָה	צָרְכִּי	גָּדְלוֹ	2.
קָדְשׁוֹ	בְּגָבְהֵי	זָכְרֵנוּ	קְרָאָנוּ	עָזְרֵנוּ	קֳדָשִׁים	3.
צָהֳרַיִם	חֹשֶׁךְ	חֹשֶׁן	אָנְיָה	צָהֳלָה	אֹשֶׁר	4.
הֹוֶה	עָוֹן	וְשָׁן	וַיַּחְשֹׁף	מֹשֶׁה	מִצְוֹת	5.
לְהַחְבִּירָה	גְּוִיָּתִי	וְהַמִּשְׂרָה	מִצְוֹתַי	חֲרָשְׁתָּן	חֲרֹשֶׁת	6.

SUPER READING SECRET

In the following words, the ◻ָ *is pronounced "oh" when it is followed by a* ◻.

Practice reading these words and phrases.

חָכְמָה בְּגָבְהֵי זָכְרֵנוּ חָפְשִׁי קָדְשׁוֹ

א. בְּחָכְ + מָה = בְּחָכְמָה

ב. וְהוּא + הָיָה + וְהוּא + הֹוֶה = וְהוּא הָיָה וְהוּא הֹוֶה

ג. וְהוּא + גּוֹאֲלִי + וְחַי + אֵלִי = וְהוּא אֵלִי וְחַי גּוֹאֲלִי

ד. לְעֵת + נַעֲשָׂה + בְּחֶפְצוֹ + כֹּל = לְעֵת נַעֲשָׂה בְּחֶפְצוֹ כֹּל

ה. בְּחָכְמָה + פּוֹתֵחַ + שְׁעָרִים = בְּחָכְמָה פּוֹתֵחַ שְׁעָרִים

The Twelve Gates

If you have ever gone to services at another synagogue, you might have noticed many differences, including different versions of some prayers. Some differences reflect the many lands in which our people have lived, while others express the ideas of various Jewish movements.

"There are twelve gates through which the prayers of Israel ascend into heaven. Each tradition has its own gate. Thus, each Israelite should pray according to his or her own tradition so as not to bring confusion into the higher realms."
(Rabbi Isaac Luria, 1534 - 1572)

The original version of אֲדוֹן עוֹלָם is longer than the one you might know. It was sung by Jews whose ancestors were forced to leave Spain in 1492. These Jews are called the Sephardim. Jews whose families come from Eastern Europe are called Ashkenazim. They omit the words that are shaded on the next page.

Some Sephardim settled in Portugal. There they developed a shorter version of אֲדוֹן עוֹלָם. When they later settled in Holland and England, they brought their version of the prayer with them.

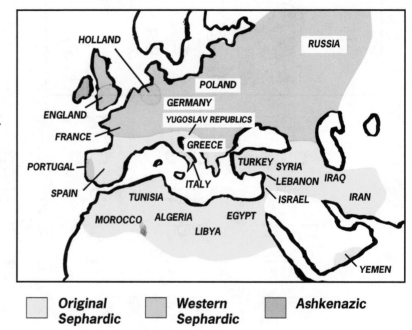

Original Sephardic

Western Sephardic

Ashkenazic

This map has been coded by the versions of אֲדוֹן עוֹלָם. Answer the questions.

1. In which countries did your ancestors live?

_____

2. What version(s) of אֲדוֹן עוֹלָם did your family originally say?

_____

Some Dutch Jews settled in the New World. When the Portuguese captured Brazil, the Jews fled back to Holland. But one group never made it home. Lost in a storm, they were captured and robbed by pirates. A French captain rescued them, and took them to New Amsterdam (New York). In September 1654, these refugees founded the first Jewish congregation in North America.

3. What version of אֲדוֹן עוֹלָם was first recited in America? _____

אֲדוֹן עוֹלָם

The Eternal One ruled	אֲדוֹן עוֹלָם, אֲשֶׁר מָלַךְ	.1
Before any being had been created.	בְּטֶרֶם כָּל־יְצִיר נִבְרָא.	.2
Once creation was done	לְעֵת נַעֲשָׂה בְחֶפְצוֹ כֹּל	.3
God's Name was known.	אֲזַי מֶלֶךְ שְׁמוֹ נִקְרָא.	.4
After everything has ceased to be	וְאַחֲרֵי כִּכְלוֹת הַכֹּל	.5
God alone will still reign.	לְבַדּוֹ יִמְלוֹךְ נוֹרָא.	.6
God was and is	וְהוּא הָיָה וְהוּא הֹוֶה	.7
And will be in glory.	וְהוּא יִהְיֶה בְּתִפְאָרָה.	.8
God is One and none other	וְהוּא אֶחָד וְאֵין שֵׁנִי	.9
Can compare to God.	לְהַמְשִׁיל לוֹ לְהַחְבִּירָה.	.10
Without beginning, without end,	בְּלִי רֵאשִׁית בְּלִי תַכְלִית	.11
To God alone is the power to rule.	וְלוֹ הָעֹז וְהַמִּשְׂרָה.	.12
Without limit, without likeness,	בְּלִי עֵרֶךְ בְּלִי דִמְיוֹן	.13
Without alteration or change.	בְּלִי שִׁנּוּי וְהַתְּמוּרָה.	.14
Without addition, without separation,	בְּלִי חִבּוּר בְּלִי פֵּרוּד	.15
Great in strength and power.	גָּדוֹל כֹּחַ וְהַגְּבוּרָה.	.16
This is my God Who saves my life,	וְהוּא אֵלִי וְחַי גּוֹאֲלִי	.17
My Rock in time of trouble.	וְצוּר חֶבְלִי (בְּעֵת צָרָה) (בְּיוֹם צָרָה) .	.18
God is my Banner and my Refuge,	וְהוּא נִסִּי וּמָנוֹס לִי	.19
Who fills my cup whenever I call.	מְנָת כּוֹסִי בְּיוֹם אֶקְרָא.	.20
God is a physician and healer	וְהוּא רוֹפֵא וְהוּא מַרְפֵּא	.21
Who watches over and helps.	וְהוּא צוֹפֶה וְהוּא עֶזְרָה.	.22
Into God's hands I place my spirit	בְּיָדוֹ אַפְקִיד רוּחִי	.23
When I sleep and when I wake.	בְּעֵת אִישַׁן וְאָעִירָה.	.24
And with my spirit, my body too.	וְעִם־רוּחִי גְּוִיָּתִי	.25
The Eternal One is with me, I shall not fear.	יְיָ לִי וְלֹא אִירָא.	.26
In God's sanctuary my soul will rejoice,	בְּמִקְדָּשׁוֹ תָּגֵל נַפְשִׁי	.27
God will send the Messiah soon.	מְשִׁיחֵנוּ יִשְׁלַח מְהֵרָה.	.28
And then we will sing in the Holy House	וְאָז נָשִׁיר בְּבֵית קָדְשִׁי	.29
Amen, Amen, Awesome is God's Name.	אָמֵן אָמֵן שֵׁם הַנּוֹרָא.	.30

☐ = *Original Sephardic phrasing*

All Around the World

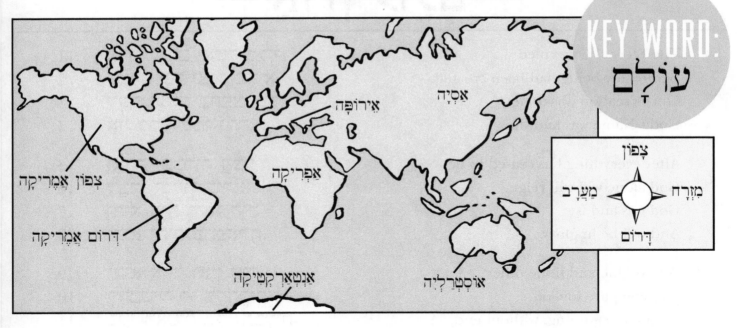

Write the following place names in the correct columns below.

גֶּרְמַנְיָה	בֶּרְלִין	בּוֹסְטוֹן	בְּאֵר שֶׁבַע	אֲלַסְקָה	שִׁיקָגוֹ
יָפוֹ	יְרוּשָׁלַיִם	טְבֶרְיָה	חֵיפָה	הוֹלַנְד	דֶּנְמַרְק
קוֹלוֹרָדוֹ	קָנָדָה	פָּרִיז	רוּסְיָה	מֶקְסִיקוֹ	לוֹנְדוֹן
תֵּל אָבִיב		קָלִיפוֹרְנְיָה		קִבּוּץ דְּגַנְיָה

בְּצָפוֹן אֲמֶרִיקָה

בְּאֵירוֹפָּה

בְּיִשְׂרָאֵל

_____

_____

_____

_____

_____

_____

_____

I Believe . . .

Complete this survey.

		YES	NO	MAYBE
1.	I believe that God existed before the universe was created	☐	☐	☐
2.	I believe that God created the universe	☐	☐	☐
3.	I believe that God rules the universe	☐	☐	☐
4.	I believe that God will exist even if the universe ends	☐	☐	☐
5.	I believe that God is unlike anyone or anything else	☐	☐	☐
6.	I believe that God is everywhere	☐	☐	☐
7.	I believe that God has no beginning and no end	☐	☐	☐
8.	I believe that God is all-powerful	☐	☐	☐
9.	I believe that God decides what is good and what is evil	☐	☐	☐
10.	I believe that God rewards good and punishes evil	☐	☐	☐
11.	I believe that prayer is an effort to talk to God	☐	☐	☐
12.	I believe that God listens to my prayers	☐	☐	☐
13.	I believe that God can answer our prayers	☐	☐	☐
14.	I believe that God knows and keeps track of what I do	☐	☐	☐
15.	I believe that God cares about me and what happens to me	☐	☐	☐
16.	I believe that God is the source of the good things in my life	☐	☐	☐
17.	I believe that God helps me when I am in trouble	☐	☐	☐
18.	I believe that God takes care of me and protects me	☐	☐	☐

> **"CONSIDER how high God is above the world!
> Yet if you enter the synagogue and stand behind a
> pillar and pray in a whisper, the Holy and Blessed
> One listens to the prayer...
> Can there be a God nearer than this, who is as
> near to us as the mouth is to the ear?"**
>
> (Jerusalem Talmud, *Berachot* 9.1)

Where Does God Live?

Yossi usually had something to say about everything. But while Mrs. Shapiro's class was discussing their ideas about God, he remained surprisingly silent.

"Is everything okay, Yossi?" Mrs. Shapiro asked. "We haven't heard from you at all today."

" I just don't believe all this stuff," Yossi answered. "God is supposed to be everywhere, right? So if God is everywhere, does that mean that God is even in my carpool?"

All of the other students laughed. Mrs. Shapiro smiled and said, "Yossi isn't the first person who's ever asked this question about God, although he may be the first to ask it about a carpool. But lots of people have wondered if there are any limits to where God can be, or why it sometimes feels like God isn't with us."

"Like if there was life on other planets," Sarah added, "would God be there too?"

"Yeah," Michael agreed. "Or if God is really everywhere, why isn't the world a better place?"

"It reminds me of a wonderful Hasidic story that may help you to find some answers to these questions," Mrs. Shapiro said. Then she told the class the following story:

Rabbi Mendel of Kotzk was famous for being very knowledgeable as well as very pious. He once asked a group of learned guests, "Where does God live?" Surprised by his question, they answered, "Is not the whole world filled with God's glory?" Rabbi Mendel shook his head and replied, "God lives wherever we invite God in."

"Hey, Yossi!" Esther called from across the room. "Maybe God could be in your carpool after all!"

YIDBIT

י-ה-ו-ה

Spinoza pointed out that this name of God is made up of three of the Hebrew words that are found in the אֲדוֹן עוֹלָם *prayer:*

יִהְיֶה   הֹוֶה   הָיָה

"Moses saw God as a Being who has always existed, does exist, and always will exist. He therefore called God יהוה*, from which the Hebrew words for past, present, and future are made."*

(Baruch Spinoza, Dutch Jewish Philosopher, 1632-1677)

How can you invite God into your carpool, your home, your classroom, or a team sport?

Language Enrichment

אוֹצָר מִלִּים
A TREASURY OF WORDS

 KEY WORD:
עוֹלָם

רוֹאֶה / רוֹאָה

> "The microscope, no less than the telescope, has revealed unknown galaxies moving in tune to the same music of the spheres — a clue to the most awesome mystery of all, which is the Divine Unity in nature."
>
> (David Sarnoff, Television Pioneer)

Complete each sentence with רוֹאֶה *or* רוֹאָה .

1. שָׂרָה _____ עוֹלָם. הִיא רוֹאָה עוֹלָם גָּדוֹל בְּטֶלֶסְקוֹפּ.

2. דָּנִיאֵל _____ עוֹלָם. הוּא רוֹאֶה עוֹלָם קָטָן בְּמִיקְרוֹסְקוֹפּ.

3. מִיכָאֵל _____ עוֹלָם. _____ רוֹאֶה עוֹלָם גָּדוֹל בְּטֶלֶסְקוֹפּ.

4. אֶסְתֵּר _____ עוֹלָם. _____ רוֹאָה עוֹלָם קָטָן בְּמִיקְרוֹסְקוֹפּ.

5. יוֹסִי לֹא _____ אֶת הָעוֹלָם.

Draw lines connecting each person's name with what he or she sees.

יוֹסִי	אֶסְתֵּר	מִיכָאֵל	דָּנִיאֵל	שָׂרָה

Language Enrichment

אֵיפֹה בָּעוֹלָם כַּרְמֶלָה יְרוּשָׁלַיִם?

Track Carmela Yerushalayim to her secret hideout in Israel. Play this game with a partner. You will have one die to roll, and a marker for each player.

DIRECTIONS

1. Begin in the square closest to where you live.
2. Each player rolls the die. The player who rolls the highest number goes first.
3. When you land on a continent for the first time, write its name in your דַּרְכּוֹן.
4. During each turn, you may move as many spaces as you wish.
   The *direction* you move will be determined by the number you roll.
5. You must spend at least one turn in each continent before you visit יִשְׂרָאֵל.
6. If you reach the edge of the map and cannot move in the direction you roll,
   return to the place you started and continue from there.
7. The winner is the one who gets to יִשְׂרָאֵל first.

HOW TO MOVE

IF YOU ROLL:

⚀ מִזְרָח

⚁ מַעֲרָב

⚂ צָפוֹן

⚃ דָּרוֹם

⚄ לָזוּז חָפְשִׁי
(Free move — go in any direction)

⚅ לֹא לָזוּז
(No moving — do not move for 1 turn)

**After you travel the world, get ready
for a different type of journey —
a journey through prayer.**

PASSPORT דַּרְכּוֹן

שֵׁם פְּרָטִי _____

שֵׁם מִשְׁפָּחָה _____

_____ .1

_____ .2

_____ .3

_____ .4

_____ .5

_____ .6

_____ .7

יִשְׂרָאֵל _____ .8

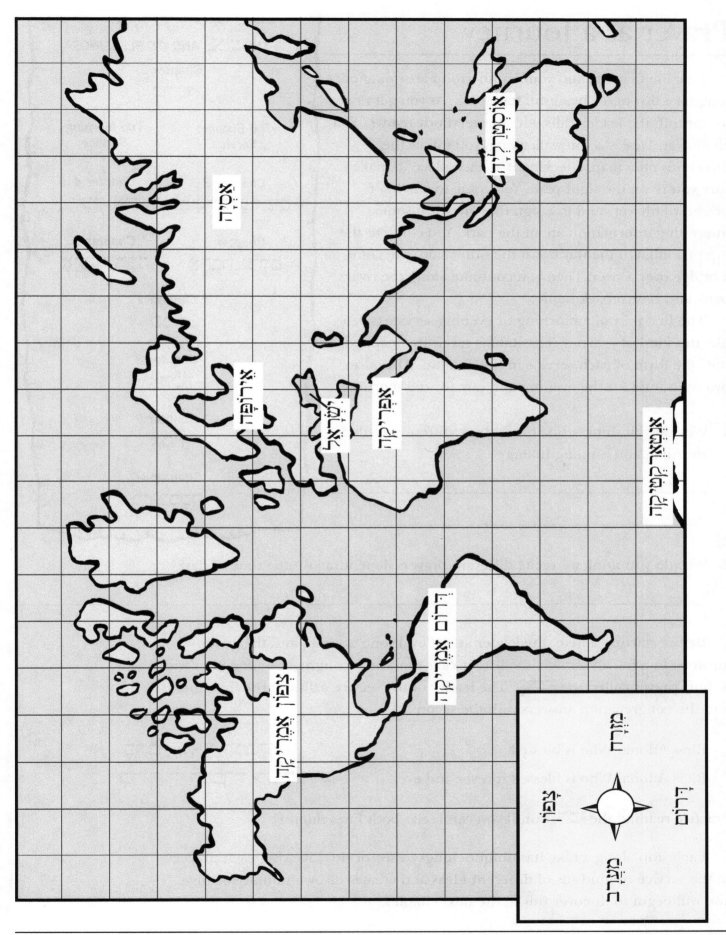

Prayer as a Journey

Imagine that you and your youth group are going on a long hike through a beautiful state park. As you get ready to start off, the leader calls out, "Is everybody ready?" You all answer, "Yes!" As you walk along, you follow the directions on a map, checking it at each place to make sure you're on the right path. You come to a field of bright wildflowers and to a sign that gives you some interesting information about the park. You climb to the top of a hill. On the way down the other side, you come to a bridge over a river. Then you continue along the river bank and return back home.

The first part of a morning or evening service is just like this kind of journey. The Rabbis carefully "mapped out" the form of each service in the Talmud. They drew two trails, one for the evening and one for the morning.

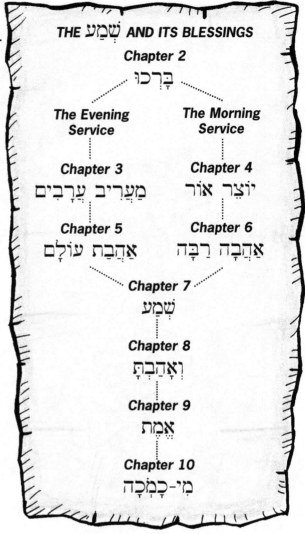

THE שְׁמַע AND ITS BLESSINGS

Chapter 2
בָּרְכוּ

The Evening Service   **The Morning Service**

Chapter 3   **Chapter 4**
מַעֲרִיב עֲרָבִים   יוֹצֵר אוֹר

Chapter 5   **Chapter 6**
אַהֲבָה רַבָּה   אַהֲבַת עוֹלָם

Chapter 7
שְׁמַע

Chapter 8
וְאָהַבְתָּ

Chapter 9
אֱמֶת

Chapter 10
מִי-כָמֹכָה

1. Why do you think a hiker might use different trails for morning and evening hiking?

   _____

   _____

2. Why do you think we recite different prayers depending on the time of day?

   _____

Before starting a hike, the leader asks if everyone is ready, and the group answers. In a Jewish service, the leader calls the whole congregation together with a short prayer called the בָּרְכוּ. The leader of the service calls out the first line, and the congregation answers with the second:

Bless Adonai Who is blessed.   1. בָּרְכוּ אֶת-יְיָ הַמְבֹרָךְ.

Bless Adonai Who is blessed forever and ever.   2. בָּרוּךְ יְיָ הַמְבֹרָךְ לְעוֹלָם וָעֶד.

Practice reading the בָּרְכוּ until you can recite both lines fluently.

Each stop along a hike has unique things to see or do. Likewise, each prayer in the service reminds us of different ideas and creates its own unique feelings. You will begin to discover this in the next chapter.

CHAPTER 3
"God Made the World with Wisdom."

מַעֲרִיב עֲרָבִים

FOCUS ON PHONICS:

לְל / מְמ

דַף קְרִיאָה
READING PAGE

KEY WORD:
עֶרֶב

1. הַלֵּל · · · · · · · הַלְלוּ · · · · · · · הַלְלוּיָהּ · · · · · · · יְהַלְלוּ · · · · · · · יְהַלְלוּךְ · · · · · · · רוֹמְמוּ

2. עֲנֵנִי · · · · · · · הִנְנִי · · · · · · · חֲגִגָּה · · · · · · · הִתְבּוֹדְדוּת · · · · · · · סְבִיבוֹן · · · · · · · מִסְתּוֹבְבִים

3. יִלְמְדוּ · · · · · · · יִשְׂמְחוּ · · · · · · · יִכְבְּשׁוּ · · · · · · · תִּזְכְּרוּ · · · · · · · יִבְטְחוּ · · · · · · · נַפְשְׁךָ

4. תִּשְׁמְרוּ · · · · · · · מִגְדְּלֵי · · · · · · · מִשְׂגְּבִי · · · · · · · מִכְרְזֵי · · · · · · · מִבְטְחֵי · · · · · · · מֶחְקְרֵי

5. חַסְדְּךָ · · · · · · · עַבְדְּךָ · · · · · · · תִּזְכְּרוּ · · · · · · · וּבְלֶכְתְּךָ · · · · · · · בְּשִׁבְתְּךָ · · · · · · · בְּמִשְׁמְרֹתֵיהֶם

6. אַרְצְכֶם · · · · · · · כְּמִשְׁפָּחוֹת · · · · · · · מִשְׁפַּחְתְּךָ · · · · · · · מִמְשַׁלְתְּךָ · · · · · · · קָדְשְׁךָ · · · · · · · וּבְשָׁכְבְּךָ

READING REMINDER

How is the [ ] pronounced when it is followed by a [ ] in the words below? _____

(Hint: You can find the answer on page 13.)

וּבְשָׁכְבְּךָ · · · · · · · קָדְשְׁךָ · · · · · · · קָדְשׁוֹ · · · · · · · חָכְמָה · · · · · · · זָכְרֵנוּ · · · · · · · חָפְשִׁי

Practice reading these prayer phrases.

א. וּמַחֲלִיף + אֶת-הַזְּמַנִים = וּמַחֲלִיף אֶת-הַזְּמַנִים

ב. וּבִתְבוּנָה + מְשַׁנֶּה + עִתִּים = וּבִתְבוּנָה מְשַׁנֶּה עִתִּים

ג. אֲשֶׁר + בִּדְבָרוֹ + מַעֲרִיב + עֲרָבִים = אֲשֶׁר בִּדְבָרוֹ מַעֲרִיב עֲרָבִים

ד. בְּחָכְמָה + פּוֹתֵחַ + שְׁעָרִים = בְּחָכְמָה פּוֹתֵחַ שְׁעָרִים

ה. בְּמִשְׁמְרוֹתֵיהֶם + בָּרָקִיעַ + כִּרְצוֹנוֹ = בְּמִשְׁמְרוֹתֵיהֶם בָּרָקִיעַ כִּרְצוֹנוֹ

Evening Stars

עֶרֶב   עֲרָבִים

"To cause sunset" = מַעֲרִיב

צָפוֹן

מַעֲרָב   מִזְרָח

דָרוֹם

עֶרֶב טוֹב, אִמָּא!

עֶרֶב טוֹב, רִבְקָה!

Words often come in families. Hebrew word families usually share three letters
that come in the same order. All the words in a word family share a related meaning.

1. What three letters do all of these words share?

מַעֲרִיב   עֲרָבִים   מַעֲרָב   ___ ___ ___

2. What is the connection between מַעֲרָב ("west") and the Key Word עֶרֶב?

_____

*Play this game with a partner. Taking turns, choose any word in the galaxy and read it.
When you read a word correctly you score the number of points above it. Each word may
be read only once per game. When all the words have been read, total your scores.*

15 הַכּוֹכָבִים

15 חֹשֶׁךְ

15 וּמַחֲלִיף

10 וּמֵבִיא

10 צְבָאוֹת

20 פּוֹתֵחַ

20 בְּחָכְמָה

15 וּבִתְבוּנָה

15 וְקַיָם

10 גּוֹלֵל

10 לַיְלָה

10 מִשְׁנֶה

25 בְּמִשְׁמְרוֹתֵיהֶם

מַעֲרִיב עֲרָבִים

Blessed are You, Adonai our God,	1. בָּרוּךְ אַתָּה יְיָ אֱלֹהֵינוּ,
Ruler of the universe,	2. מֶלֶךְ הָעוֹלָם,
Whose word brings on the evening,	3. אֲשֶׁר בִּדְבָרוֹ מַעֲרִיב עֲרָבִים,
Whose wisdom opens the gates,	4. בְּחָכְמָה פּוֹתֵחַ שְׁעָרִים,
Whose intelligence makes the ages pass	5. וּבִתְבוּנָה מְשַׁנֶּה עִתִּים,
And the seasons change,	6. וּמַחֲלִיף אֶת־הַזְּמַנִּים,
And Who arranges the stars	7. וּמְסַדֵּר אֶת־הַכּוֹכָבִים
In their places in the sky.	8. בְּמִשְׁמְרוֹתֵיהֶם בָּרָקִיעַ כִּרְצוֹנוֹ.
Creator of day and night,	9. בּוֹרֵא יוֹם וָלַיְלָה,
Rolling light before darkness	10. גּוֹלֵל אוֹר מִפְּנֵי חֹשֶׁךְ
And darkness before light,	11. וְחֹשֶׁךְ מִפְּנֵי אוֹר,
Causing day to pass and bringing on the night,	12. וּמַעֲבִיר יוֹם וּמֵבִיא לָיְלָה,
Separating day from night,	13. וּמַבְדִּיל בֵּין יוֹם וּבֵין לָיְלָה,
The Commander of Heaven is God's name.	14. יְיָ צְבָאוֹת שְׁמוֹ.
May the living and enduring God	15. אֵל חַי וְקַיָּם,
Rule over us always and forever.	16. תָּמִיד יִמְלוֹךְ עָלֵינוּ לְעוֹלָם וָעֶד.
Blessed are You, Eternal One,	17. בָּרוּךְ אַתָּה יְיָ,
Whose word makes evening fall.	18. הַמַּעֲרִיב עֲרָבִים.

Study the מַעֲרִיב עֲרָבִים **and its translation.**

Then answer questions about the images found in this prayer.

1. What English words and phrases in the first two sections tell us that this prayer is said at night?

   _____

2. What words in the first section tell us that God created the world with care and thought?

   _____

Science, Wonder, and Wisdom

TEST YOUR ASTRONOMY KNOWLEDGE: A QUIZ

Check the box next to the correct answer.

1. The earth is . . .
   - ❏ the center of the universe
   - ❏ the third planet from our sun
   - ❏ flat
2. The Milky Way is . . .
   - ❏ the galaxy in which our solar system is located
   - ❏ a delicious candy bar
3. Planets . . .
   - ❏ move randomly in space
   - ❏ have orbits around stars

4. The sun rises and sets because . . .
   - ❏ the earth rotates on its axis once every 24 hours
   - ❏ the sun orbits the earth
5. The seasons change . . .
   - ❏ so we don't have to watch football all year long
   - ❏ because the earth tilts on its axis as it orbits the sun

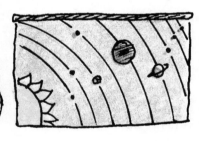

"Why are we talking about science in Hebrew school?" Yossi asked before everyone managed to finish the quiz. "Aren't we supposed to be learning about prayer and religion?"

"Good question!" Mrs. Shapiro said. "The wonders of science and nature are very important in the Jewish tradition. The Torah teaches us that God created and controls the universe. Both science and Judaism help us understand the universe. They just do it in different ways."

"But they don't always agree, right?" asked Esther. "I mean, we've been learning about that stuff in my science class, and the teacher said that it took millions of years for the universe to be created and for life to develop on earth. But the Torah says it only took six days. Which one is true?"

Mrs. Shapiro smiled. "I'm so glad you brought that up, Esther. Maybe they are both true, but in different ways." But before she could explain, the bell rang. "In fact, I have a worksheet for you on just this topic for your homework. We'll discuss your answers next time."

Everyone groaned as they closed their books, grabbed a worksheet, and raced for their carpools.

Mrs. Shapiro's Homework

Check each answer that you think makes the statements true.

Science gives us information about the universe that:

❑ is factual

❑ is based on things we can observe

❑ is based on the results of experiments

❑ is based on things we feel or believe

❑ explains how the universe was created

❑ explains why the universe was created

❑ is full of wisdom

❑ fills us with a sense of wonder

Judaism gives us information about the universe that:

❑ is factual

❑ is based on things we can observe

❑ is based on the results of experiments

❑ is based on things we feel or believe

❑ explains how the universe was created

❑ explains why the universe was created

❑ is full of wisdom

❑ fills us with a sense of wonder

Unscramble the words to find words from the מַעֲרִיב עֲרָבִים prayer.

(Hint: You can find all of these words on page 25.)

רוֹא

תֵעִים

יְלָלַה

עוֹהָלָם

בְּקִירָע

רְבִיעֶם

רִישְׁעָם

כּוֹבִיכֶהֶם

"Science too, springs from God, and
differs from Torah only in subject matter."
(Rabbi Yehuda Loew, 1525–1609)

TEXT EXploration

Prayer is a special kind of poetry. It uses poetic images to express thoughts and feelings. Poetic images paint a picture in our minds by comparing one thing with another. The prayer מַעֲרִיב עֲרָבִים contains a very interesting poetic image.

Complete the translation.

שְׁעָרִים

שַׁעַר

"with wisdom (God) opens _____"

בְּחָכְמָה פּוֹתֵחַ שְׁעָרִים

Have you ever seen God open a gate?

❑ Yes   ❑ No

Maybe the שְׁעָרִים are not actual gates.

So . . . the word שְׁעָרִים is used in this prayer as:

❑ a word meaning "doors in a wall"

❑ a poetic image for sunset

❑ the plural of gate

How are sunset and sunrise like gates? _____

What is being let in or out? _____

Our tradition talks about many kinds of gates. Fill in the blanks below:

_____ OF HEAVEN

שַׁעֲרֵי שָׁמַיִם

_____ OF REPENTANCE

סְלִיחָה   סְלִיחָה

שַׁעֲרֵי תְּשׁוּבָה

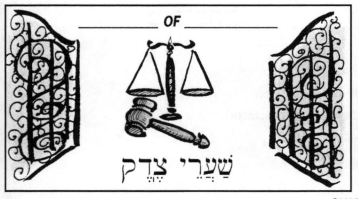

_____ OF _____

שַׁעֲרֵי צֶדֶק

_____ _____ _____

שַׁעֲרֵי תְּפִלָּה

Language Enrichment

אוֹצַר מִלִּים
A TREASURY OF WORDS

עֶרֶב

לַיְלָה

עֲרָבִים

אוֹר

חֹשֶׁךְ

כּוֹכָב

כּוֹכָבִים

שֶׁמֶשׁ

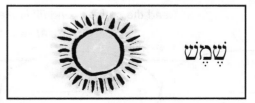

יָרֵחַ

Draw a line from each word to its picture.

יָרֵחַ		בֹּקֶר
אוֹר		שֶׁמֶשׁ
יוֹם		כּוֹכָבִים
לַיְלָה		חֹשֶׁךְ

Language Enrichment

זְמַן, זְמַן, זְמַן

What do Daniel and Esther see through their windows?
In the windows, draw the time of day that matches their greetings.

Complete the sentences.

מַה דָּנִיאֵל רוֹאֶה?

הוּא רוֹאֶה_____ וְ_____.

מָה אֶסְתֵּר רוֹאָה?

הִיא רוֹאָה_____, _____ וְ_____.

מָה אַתָּה רוֹאֶה? / מָה אַתְּ רוֹאָה?

_____.

Read the captions and fill in the balloons with the correct greetings.
Answer the questions.

עַל הַשֻּׁלְחָן, אֶסְתֵּר רוֹאָה בֵּיגֶל,
קוֹרְנְפְלֵקְס, מֶלוֹן, וְתֵה.

עַל הַשֻּׁלְחָן, דָּנִיאֵל רוֹאֶה הַמְבּוּרְגֶר,
עִם קֶטְשׁוּפּ, סָלָט, וְלִמוֹנָדָה.

The More the Merrier

Draw in the missing parts of each picture. The first one has been completed.

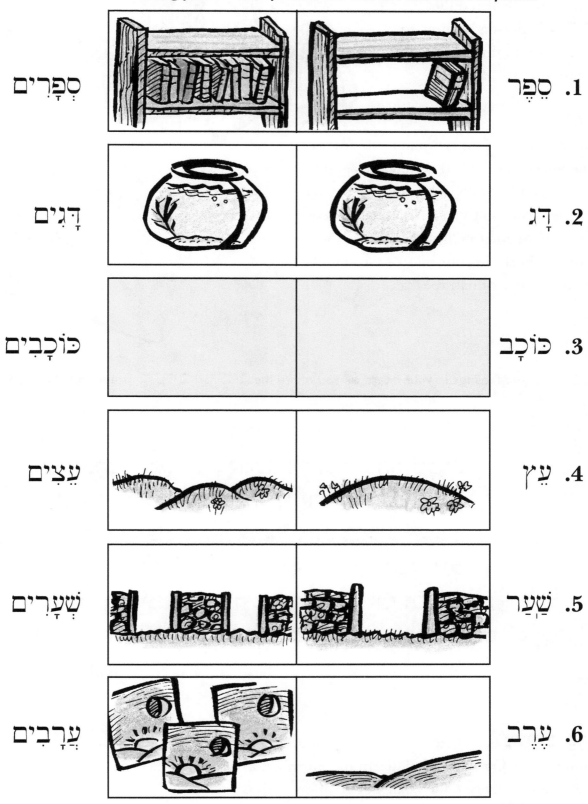

1. סֵפֶר — סְפָרִים

2. דָג — דָגִים

3. כּוֹכָב — כּוֹכָבִים

4. עֵץ — עֵצִים

5. שַׁעַר — שְׁעָרִים

6. עֶרֶב — עֲרָבִים

All of the words above are masculine. Most of the time, Hebrew masculine nouns can be made plural by attaching the suffix _____ .

"You Awe Here"

Now that you've learned the מַעֲרִיב עֲרָבִים prayer, it's time to give some thought to this part of your Prayer Journey.

Imagine that you are an astronaut orbiting the earth in the Space Shuttle "Merkavah." It's evening. You turn away from your console and gaze out the window at the vastness of space. You see the earth, like a blue jewel, floating below you. Picture the beauty of the night sky in your mind's eye and think about the importance of nature.

Keep these images and feelings in your heart, as you recite the מַעֲרִיב עֲרָבִים **prayer quietly to yourself.**

בָּרוּךְ אַתָּה יְיָ, אֱלֹהֵינוּ מֶלֶךְ הָעוֹלָם,

אֲשֶׁר בִּדְבָרוֹ מַעֲרִיב עֲרָבִים, בְּחָכְמָה פּוֹתֵחַ שְׁעָרִים,

וּבִתְבוּנָה מְשַׁנֶּה עִתִּים, וּמַחֲלִיף אֶת-הַזְּמַנִּים,

וּמְסַדֵּר אֶת-הַכּוֹכָבִים בְּמִשְׁמְרוֹתֵיהֶם בָּרָקִיעַ כִּרְצוֹנוֹ.

בּוֹרֵא יוֹם וָלַיְלָה, גּוֹלֵל אוֹר מִפְּנֵי חֹשֶׁךְ וְחֹשֶׁךְ מִפְּנֵי אוֹר,

וּמַעֲבִיר יוֹם וּמֵבִיא לָיְלָה, וּמַבְדִּיל בֵּין יוֹם וּבֵין לָיְלָה,

יְיָ צְבָאוֹת שְׁמוֹ. אֵל חַי וְקַיָּם, תָּמִיד יִמְלוֹךְ עָלֵינוּ לְעוֹלָם וָעֶד.

בָּרוּךְ אַתָּה יְיָ, הַמַּעֲרִיב עֲרָבִים.

The מַעֲרִיב עֲרָבִים is recited in the evening. It describes the beauty found as evening turns to night. In the morning, a different prayer is recited to celebrate the beauty of creation. This prayer, the יוֹצֵר אוֹר, is what you will study next.

CHAPTER **4**
"God Creates the World Every Day"

Lights, Camera, Action!

KEY WORD:
אוֹר

SCENE 1

Time: _____
Place: _____
Description: _____

SCENE 2

Time: _____
Place: _____
Description: _____

How is Scene 2 different from Scene 1? What changed?

_____

וּבְטוּבוֹ מְחַדֵּשׁ בְּכָל-יוֹם תָּמִיד מַעֲשֵׂה בְרֵאשִׁית.

"In goodness God renews the work of creation every day."

The Talmud teaches us that the world was not just created once, but that God is continuously recreating it. This idea is also found in the יוֹצֵר אוֹר prayer. How do you think God renews the work of creation every day?

_____

Let There Be Light

Practice reading these phrases.

כֻּלָם בְּחָכְמָה עָשִׂיתָ   כֻּלָם + בְּחָכְמָה + עָשִׂיתָ =

עַל־שֶׁבַח מַעֲשֵׂה יָדֶיךָ   עַל־שֶׁבַח + מַעֲשֵׂה + יָדֶיךָ =

יוֹצֵר אוֹר וּבוֹרֵא חֹשֶׁךְ   יוֹצֵר + אוֹר + וּבוֹרֵא + חֹשֶׁךְ =

עֹשֶׂה שָׁלוֹם וּבוֹרֵא אֶת־הַכֹּל   עֹשֶׂה + שָׁלוֹם + וּבוֹרֵא + אֶת־הַכֹּל =

וְעַל־מְאוֹרֵי־אוֹר שֶׁעָשִׂיתָ   וְעַל־מְאוֹרֵי־אוֹר + שֶׁעָשִׂיתָ =

וּבְטוּבוֹ מְחַדֵּשׁ בְּכָל־יוֹם תָּמִיד   וּבְטוּבוֹ + מְחַדֵּשׁ + בְּכָל־יוֹם + תָּמִיד =

1. Circle the Key Word.   1. וְעַל־מְאוֹרֵי־אוֹר שֶׁעָשִׂיתָ

2. Circle the word that does not have an S sound in it.   2. מַעֲשֵׂה בְּרֵאשִׁית

3. Circle the words that have a T sound in them.   3. וּבְטוּבוֹ מְחַדֵּשׁ בְּכָל־יוֹם תָּמִיד

4. Circle the word that has an S sound in it.   4. עֹשֶׂה שָׁלוֹם וּבוֹרֵא אֶת־הַכֹּל

5. Circle the word that has an S sound in it.   5. עַל־שֶׁבַח מַעֲשֵׂה יָדֶיךָ

6. Some dots do a double duty in Hebrew.   6. יוֹצֵר אוֹר וּבוֹרֵא חֹשֶׁךְ
   Circle the word that has a "double duty" dot.

Fill in the answer words to complete the blessing said for seeing beautiful things in nature.

בָּרוּךְ אַתָּה יְיָ אֱלֹהֵינוּ, מֶלֶךְ הָעוֹלָם, _____ _____ _____.

    2   5   4

Blessed are You Adonai our God, Ruler of the Universe, Who makes the wonders of creation.

Help the אוֹר Reach the Earth from the שֶׁמֶשׁ

Play this game with one or two friends. Each person selects a ray of sunlight. Starting at the שֶׁמֶשׁ, take turns reading the words in your ray of light. If you make a mistake, you must return to the שֶׁמֶשׁ. The first to arrive at הָאָרֶץ is the winner.

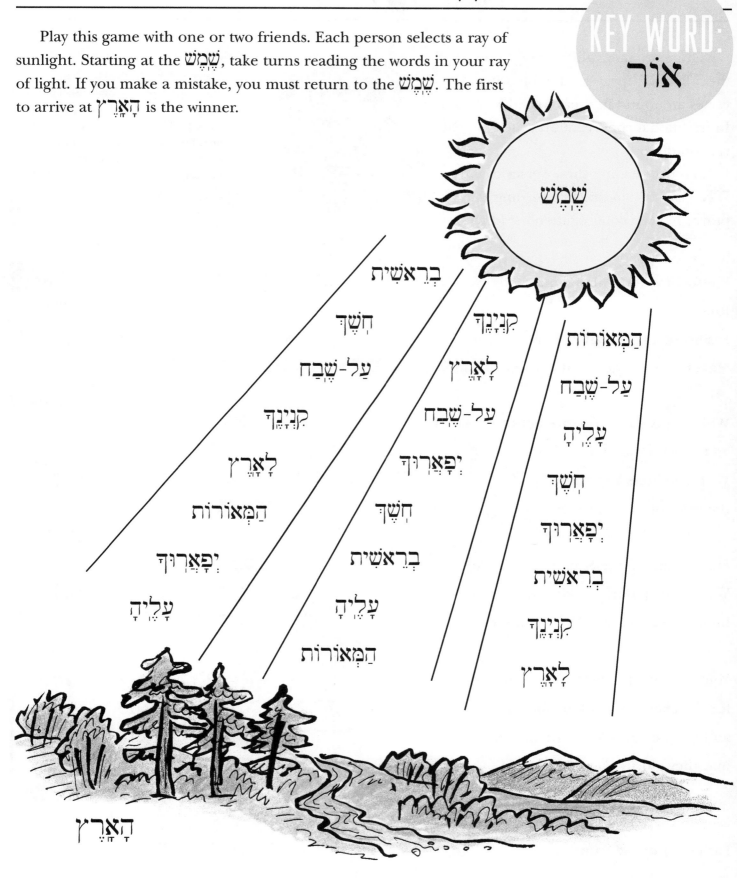

CHAPTER **4**

יוֹצֵר אוֹר

There are many different versions of the יוֹצֵר אוֹר prayer. The following verses are found in every weekday version. In traditional congregations, the Shabbat version differs.

Practice reading these verses of the יוֹצֵר אוֹר. Then practice reading this prayer in your congregation's siddur.

"There are twelve gates through which the prayers of Israel ascend into heaven. Each tradition has its own gate. Thus, each Israelite should pray according to his or her own tradition so as not to bring confusion into the higher realms."

(Rabbi Isaac Luria, 1534 - 1572)

Blessed are You, Adonai our God,	1. בָּרוּךְ אַתָּה יְיָ אֱלֹהֵינוּ,
Ruler of the universe,	2. מֶלֶךְ הָעוֹלָם,
Fashioner of light and Creator of darkness	3. יוֹצֵר אוֹר וּבוֹרֵא חְשֶׁךְ,
Maker of wholeness and Creator of all things.	4. עֹשֶׂה שָׁלוֹם וּבוֹרֵא אֶת-הַכֹּל.

With compassion You give light to the earth	5. הַמֵּאִיר לָאָרֶץ
and all who live there,	6. וְלַדָּרִים עָלֶיהָ בְּרַחֲמִים,
With goodness You renew	7. וּבְטוּבוֹ מְחַדֵּשׁ בְּכָל-יוֹם תָּמִיד
the work of creation every day.	8. מַעֲשֵׂה בְרֵאשִׁית.

How abundant are Your creations, Adonai!	9. מָה רַבּוּ מַעֲשֶׂיךָ, יְיָ!
You made all of them with wisdom,	10. כֻּלָּם בְּחָכְמָה עָשִׂיתָ,
filling the earth with Your creatures.	11. מָלְאָה הָאָרֶץ קִנְיָנֶךָ.

You shall be praised, Eternal our God,	12. תִּתְבָּרַךְ, יְיָ אֱלֹהֵינוּ,
for the excellent work of Your hands,	13. עַל-שֶׁבַח מַעֲשֵׂה יָדֶיךָ,
and for the lights You have made:	14. וְעַל-מְאוֹרֵי-אוֹר שֶׁעָשִׂיתָ:
may they glorify You forever.	15. יְפָאֲרוּךָ סֶּלָה.

Blessed are You Adonai,	16. בָּרוּךְ אַתָּה יְיָ,
Fashioner of the lights.	17. יוֹצֵר הַמְּאוֹרוֹת.

Language Enrichment

בְּרֵאשִׁית בָּרָא אֱלֹהִים

The יוֹצֵר אוֹר prayer is about creation. The Torah begins with the story of God creating the world. What can you see in this picture of גַּן עֵדֶן (the Garden of Eden)?

There is / are = יֵשׁ   There isn't / aren't = אֵין

Fill in the blanks with יֵשׁ or אֵין.

6. _____ קֶנְגּוּרוּ תַּחַת הַשֶּׁמֶשׁ.	1. _____ עֵץ גָּדוֹל.
7. _____ כּוֹכָבִים.	2. _____ חָתוּל עַל־יַד הָעֵץ.
8. _____ גּוֹרִילָה עַל־יַד הָעֵץ.	3. _____ שֶׁמֶשׁ.
9. _____ צִפּוֹר בָּעֵץ.	4. _____ דָּג בַּמַּיִם.
	5. _____ הִיפּוֹ עַל־יַד הַמַּיִם.

The יוֹצֵר אוֹר prayer is also about time.
Turn the page to learn some Hebrew words about different times.

Language Enrichment

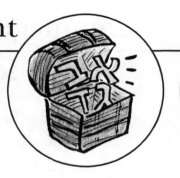

אוֹצַר מִלִים
A TREASURY OF WORDS

KEY WORD:
אוֹר

הַחֳדָשִׁים בַּלוּחַ הַיְהוּדִי

←

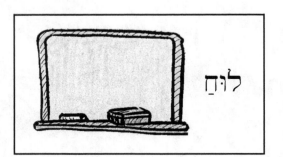

לוּחַ

לוּחַ

→

←

↑

↓

Complete the chart with the months of the Jewish year.

	קַיִץ		אָבִיב
	תַּמּוּז		נִיסָן
	_____		_____
	_____		_____
חֹרֶף		**סְתָיו**	
	טֵבֵת		_____
	_____		חֶשְׁוָן
	_____		_____

The Jewish Year

חֹרֶף

סְתָיו

אָבִיב

קַיִץ

Read the names of the special days listed below. Show which days occur in which seasons by either drawing the day's symbol or writing its Hebrew name in the boxes above.

סֻכּוֹת	חֲנֻכָּה	שַׁבָּת
יוֹם הַשּׁוֹאָה	ט״וּ בִּשְׁבָט	יוֹם כִּפּוּר
יוֹם הַהֻלֶּדֶת שֶׁלִּי	פּוּרִים	רֹאשׁ הַשָּׁנָה
שִׂמְחַת תּוֹרָה	תִּשְׁעָה בְּאָב	שָׁבוּעוֹת
יוֹם הָעַצְמָאוּת	פֶּסַח	

"When?" = ? מָתַי

1. Read the Hebrew sentences on the facing page. For each picture below, write the number of the sentence(s) that describe it.

2. Draw a line from each picture to the matching month on the Jewish calendar.

1. יֵשׁ תּוֹרָה בַּיָּד שֶׁל הַמּוֹרָה בְּשִׂמְחַת תּוֹרָה. יֵשׁ דֶּגֶל בַּיָּד שֶׁל מִיכָאֵל בְּשִׂמְחַת תּוֹרָה. יֵשׁ דֶּגֶל בַּיָּד שֶׁל רִבְקָה בְּשִׂמְחַת תּוֹרָה. שִׂמְחַת תּוֹרָה חַג שָׂמֵחַ בְּחֹדֶשׁ תִּשְׁרֵי.

2. יֵשׁ שׁוֹפָר בַּיָּד שֶׁל הָרַבִּי בְּרֹאשׁ הַשָּׁנָה. רֹאשׁ הַשָּׁנָה חַג גָּדוֹל בְּחֹדֶשׁ תִּשְׁרֵי.

3. הַמִּשְׁפָּחָה בַּסֵּדֶר שֶׁל פֶּסַח. פֶּסַח חַג גָּדוֹל בְּחֹדֶשׁ נִיסָן.

4. בְּסֻכּוֹת אַבָּא וְדָנִי בְּסֻכָּה.

5. יֵשׁ לוּלָב וְאֶתְרוֹג בַּיָּד שֶׁל אִמָּא בְּסֻכּוֹת. סֻכּוֹת חַג גָּדוֹל בְּחֹדֶשׁ תִּשְׁרֵי.

6. יוֹסִי רוֹאֶה עֵץ בְּט״וּ בִּשְׁבָט. ט״וּ בִּשְׁבָט חַג שָׂמֵחַ בְּחֹדֶשׁ שְׁבָט.

7. אֵין לֶחֶם וְאֵין מַיִם בְּיוֹם כִּפּוּר. יוֹם כִּפּוּר חַג גָּדוֹל בְּחֹדֶשׁ תִּשְׁרֵי.

8. יֵשׁ רַעֲשָׁן בַּיָּד שֶׁל הַיֶּלֶד בְּחַג הַפּוּרִים. יֵשׁ רַעֲשָׁן בַּיָּד שֶׁל הַיַּלְדָּה בְּחַג הַפּוּרִים. פּוּרִים חַג שָׂמֵחַ בְּחֹדֶשׁ אֲדָר.

9. רוּתִי רוֹאָה חֲנֻכִּיָּה בַּחֲנֻכָּה. חֲנֻכָּה חַג שָׂמֵחַ בָּחֳדָשִׁים כִּסְלֵו וְטֵבֵת.

Yidbit

The word יֵצֶר (impulse) is related to the word יוֹצֵר.
What three letters do these two words share? _____ _____ _____

The Rabbis believed that human beings are caught up in a constant battle within themselves between two powerful forces. They called these forces:

Evil _____ = יֵצֶר הָרַע   &   _____ Impulse = יֵצֶר הַטוֹב

Read each situation. Check the box that shows which force was stronger in each person.

1. Esther finds a gold necklace on the school playground.
   She turns it into the "lost and found."

   ☐ יֵצֶר הָרַע   ☐ יֵצֶר הַטוֹב

2. At Little League practice, Danny sees his coach drop a dollar bill.
   Danny picks it up and puts it in his own pocket.

   ☐ יֵצֶר הָרַע   ☐ יֵצֶר הַטוֹב

3. Danny's little brother, Josh, keeps running through
   the court while Danny and his friends are playing
   basketball. Danny invites Josh to join in the game.

   ☐ יֵצֶר הָרַע   ☐ יֵצֶר הַטוֹב

4. Esther's little sister, Tammy, keeps running off with the
   markers while Esther and her friends are working on an art
   project. Esther yells at Tammy and calls her a "stupid baby."

   ☐ יֵצֶר הָרַע   ☐ יֵצֶר הַטוֹב

Seeing Things in a New Light

Now that you've arrived at this part of your journey, take a minute to think about the יוֹצֵר אוֹר prayer.

Imagine that you are a film maker. In celebration of Earth Day, you have been invited to make a movie about the beauty of our planet. Close your eyes, and picture some of the scenes from your movie, then answer the questions.

1. What places would you show in your movie?

_____

2. What plants and animals might you include?

_____

3. How would you show the passage of time?

_____

4. What message would you most like to communicate about our earth?

_____

Imagine that you are viewing your movie while you recite the יוֹצֵר אוֹר prayer quietly to yourself.

בָּרוּךְ אַתָּה יְיָ אֱלֹהֵינוּ, מֶלֶךְ הָעוֹלָם, יוֹצֵר אוֹר וּבוֹרֵא חֹשֶׁךְ, עֹשֶׂה שָׁלוֹם
וּבוֹרֵא אֶת-הַכֹּל. הַמֵּאִיר לָאָרֶץ וְלַדָּרִים עָלֶיהָ בְּרַחֲמִים, וּבְטוּבוֹ מְחַדֵּשׁ
בְּכָל-יוֹם תָּמִיד מַעֲשֵׂה בְרֵאשִׁית. מָה רַבּוּ מַעֲשֶׂיךָ, יְיָ! כֻּלָּם בְּחָכְמָה עָשִׂיתָ,
מָלְאָה הָאָרֶץ קִנְיָנֶךָ. תִּתְבָּרַךְ, יְיָ אֱלֹהֵינוּ, עַל-שֶׁבַח מַעֲשֵׂה יָדֶיךָ,
וְעַל-מְאוֹרֵי-אוֹר שֶׁעָשִׂיתָ: יְפָאֲרוּךָ סֶּלָה. בָּרוּךְ אַתָּה יְיָ, יוֹצֵר הַמְּאוֹרוֹת.

According to a midrash, Adam and Eve were forced out of the Garden of Eden just after Shabbat had ended. The angels gave them seeds to plant, and sweet spices to lift their spirits. God also gave them a special gift, the Torah. "Only hold fast to this Tree of Life," God said, "and soon you will find yourselves back in Paradise."

Now that you know how important creation is to us, it's time to learn how the Torah can be our own "Tree of Life."

Esther's Dream

Mrs. Shapiro looked up from taking attendance. "Esther, are you alright?"

"Sorry, Mrs. Shapiro," Esther stretched and yawned again. "I didn't get too much sleep last night."

"Out partying too much or just doing all your homework?" Yossi asked.

"Oh get a grip," Esther snapped. "Actually, I had this really weird dream, and I couldn't get back to sleep afterward."

"What did you dream?" Sarah asked.

"Well, it was like there were no rules or laws or anything."

"Cool!" Danny called out.

"At first, I thought it would be cool, too," Esther continued. "No one told me to go to bed or even to do my homework. Nobody grounded me if I stayed out all night. I got to have doughnuts and root beer for breakfast, and at school the teachers didn't care what we did in class, or even if we went to class."

Yossi jumped up and shouted. "I could go for that!"

Mrs. Shapiro stared him back into his seat. "Trust me on this, Yossi; it was only a dream." She turned back to Esther. "You said that you thought it would be cool at first. What made you change your mind?"

"That was the weird part," Esther continued. "There were no laws for anybody. The biggest bullies owned the school playground. The teachers just showed videos, and let people copy each other's answers even on tests. Drivers were running people down in the street or just smashing into each other. It was a mess!"

"I hate rules," Yossi said. "There's always like a zillion of them, and if you accidentally break even the smallest one, you get grounded for a week."

"I don't mind the part about the tests," Rebecca quietly added, "but the part about the drivers is really scary."

"That, I think is the point," Mrs. Shapiro said. "If you think about it, most rules and laws are there for a good reason, either to protect us or to help us treat others the way we'd like to be treated. The Torah is full of laws. They're called מִצְוֹת."

"I know," Michael said. "There are 613 of them in the Torah."

"That's right," Mrs. Shapiro smiled. "In fact, the prayer that we are going to be studying today makes the same point as Esther's dream. It tells us that God shows love for us the same way that our parents do: by giving us rules."

"Oh no," Yossi grumbled. "Does that mean that God is going to ground me for a week, too? I'm in real trouble!"

Esther's "dream day" without rules was more of a nightmare.
As hard as it is to believe, most rules are there for our own good.
Match each rule below to the good reason for it.

____ Eat a nutritious breakfast.

____ Stop at red lights.

____ Do not pick on smaller kids.

____ Teachers should teach.

____ Do not share test answers.

a. You do not like others to bully you.

b. Not doing your job is a kind of stealing.

c. You will have energy and be healthy..

d. People should be responsible for their work.

e. Traffic accidents can harm people.

תּוֹרָה וּמִצְוֹת חֻקִּים וּמִשְׁפָּטִים

The אַהֲבַת עוֹלָם prayer is about the rules that God has given us.
Practice reading these words from the אַהֲבַת עוֹלָם prayer,
and some other words that are related to them.

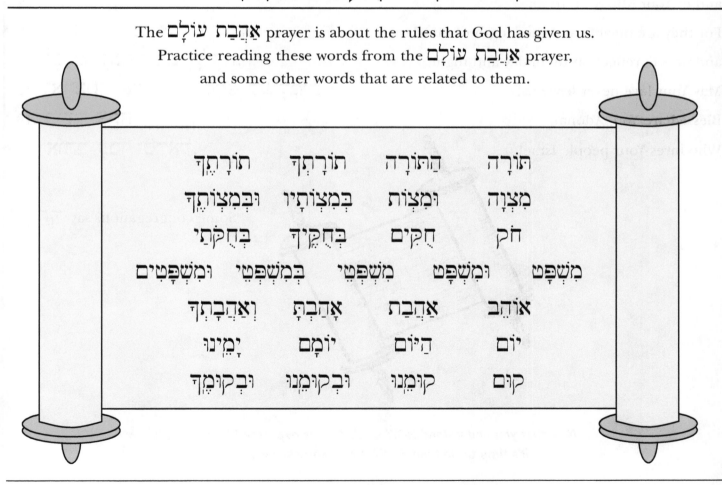

תּוֹרָתֶךָ	תּוֹרָתְךָ	הַתּוֹרָה	תּוֹרָה
וּבְמִצְוֹתֶךָ	בְּמִצְוֹתָיו	וּמִצְוֹת	מִצְוָה
בְּחֻקֹּתַי	בְּחֻקֶּיךָ	חֻקִּים	חֹק
וּמִשְׁפָּטֶיךָ	בְּמִשְׁפָּטֵי	מִשְׁפָּטֵי	וּמִשְׁפָּט	מִשְׁפָּט
וְאָהַבְתָּ	אָהַבְתָּ	אַהֲבַת	אוֹהֵב
יָמֵינוּ	יוֹמָם	הַיּוֹם	יוֹם
וּבְקוּמֶךָ	וּבְקוּמֵנוּ	קוּמֵנוּ	קוּם

אַהֲבַת עוֹלָם

Eternal is Your love for the House of Israel	1. אַהֲבַת עוֹלָם בֵּית יִשְׂרָאֵל
Your people You have loved.	2. עַמְּךָ אָהָבְתָּ.
Torah and Mitzvot, laws and judgments	3. תּוֹרָה וּמִצְוֹת, חֻקִּים וּמִשְׁפָּטִים
You have taught us.	4. אוֹתָנוּ לִמַּדְתָּ.
Therefore, Adonai our God,	5. עַל־כֵּן, יְיָ אֱלֹהֵינוּ,
when we lie down and when we rise up,	6. בְּשָׁכְבֵּנוּ וּבְקוּמֵנוּ,
we will discuss Your laws,	7. נָשִׂיחַ בְּחֻקֶּיךָ,
and rejoice in the words of Your Torah	8. וְנִשְׂמַח בְּדִבְרֵי תוֹרָתְךָ* וּבְמִצְוֹתֶיךָ
and in Your Mitzvot forever.	9. לְעוֹלָם וָעֶד.
For they are our life and the length of our days,	10. כִּי הֵם חַיֵּינוּ וְאֹרֶךְ יָמֵינוּ,
and we will reflect on them day and night.	11. וּבָהֶם נֶהְגֶּה יוֹמָם וָלָיְלָה.
May Your love never leave us!	12. וְאַהֲבָתְךָ אַל־תָּסִיר מִמֶּנּוּ לְעוֹלָמִים!
Blessed are You, Adonai,	13. בָּרוּךְ אַתָּה יְיָ,
Who loves Your people Israel.	14. אוֹהֵב עַמּוֹ יִשְׂרָאֵל.

*Some congregations say תּוֹרָתֶךָ

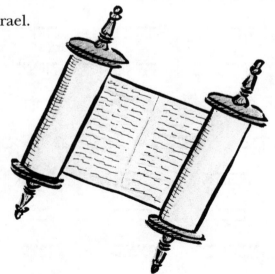

*Now that you understand HOW God's love is expressed in the Torah,
it's time to find out WHEN God expresses love for us.*

Time After Time

When does God show love for us? Fill in the missing words from the prayer phrases, then unscramble the circled letters to find the times of day.

KEY WORDS:

תּוֹרָה וּמִצְוֹת

וּבָהֶם ____ ____ ◯ ____ ____ ____ וָלַיְלָה

כִּי הֵם חַיֵּינוּ ____ ____ ____ ◯ ____ ____ יָמֵינוּ

____ ____ ◯ ◯ ____ ◯ וּמִצְוֹת, ____ וּמִשְׁפָּטִים

וְנִשְׂמַח ____ ◯ ____ ◯ ____ ◯ ____ תּוֹרָתְךָ וּבְמִצְוֹתֶיךָ

אַהֲבַת ____ ◯ ____ ◯ ____ בֵּית ____ ◯ ____ עַמְּךָ אָהָבְתָּ.

____ ____ ____ ____ . ____ ____ ____ ____ ____ ____ ____ ____
ָ   :   ֵ   ֶ   ְ   ֵ

Label all of the items in the pictures with the correct Hebrew words.
Then fill in the season and time of day captions for each picture.

שַׁעַר   שֶׁמֶשׁ   בֹּקֶר   יְרוּשָׁלַיִם   לַיְלָה
יָרֵחַ   אָבִיב   סְתָו   חֹרֶף   כּוֹכָבִים   עֵץ   עֶרֶב

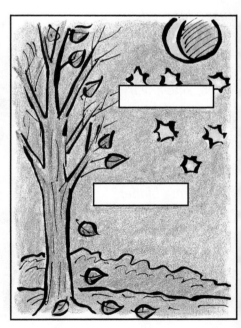

Season: _____   Season: _____   Season: _____

Time of Day: _____   Time of Day: _____   Time of Day: _____

47   CHAPTER 5

The Stylish Torah

Because the Torah is our most precious possession, it is customary to "dress it up" with elegant garments and ornaments. Here are some of the items that can be used to beautify the Torah. Match each decoration to its place on one of the scrolls.

מְעִיל
Soft cover that fits over the Torah scroll like a "tunic."

עֵץ חַיִּים
Literally a "Tree of Life"; a wooden roller to which each end of the rolled Ashkenazic scroll is attached.

יָד
Special pointer used for reading the Torah; usually shaped like a "hand"; made of gold, silver, ivory, or fine wood.

אַבְנֵט
"Belt" or "binder" that holds the rolled Ashkenazic scroll together.

כֶּתֶר
A crown, usually made of silver and placed on top of the wooden rollers.

חֹשֶׁן
Breastplate sometimes hung around the Torah. In the days of the ancient Temple, the High Priest wore a breastplate.

רִמּוֹנִים
Silver ornaments that rest on top of the wooden rollers. They often have small bells made of silver, that jingle as the Torah is carried. The name means "pomegranates."

תִּיק
Hard case made of fine wood or silver that houses a Sephardic Torah scroll.

Plenty of Plurals

Read the word and look at each picture on the right side.
Then read the word on the left and circle the picture that matches it.

1. All of the words above are: ❑ masculine   ❑ feminine

2. Hebrew masculine nouns can <u>usually</u> be made plural by attaching the suffix _____ .

3. Hebrew feminine plural nouns <u>usually</u> end in the suffix ות. For example,
   סֻכָּה = one sukkah
   סֻכּוֹת = more than one sukkah

Circle the picture that goes with each plural word.

4. All of the words above are: ❑ masculine   ❑ feminine

Torah, Torah, Torah

עִם = with

יֶלֶד עִם סֵפֶר תּוֹרָה

בְּלִי = without

יֶלֶד בְּלִי סֵפֶר תּוֹרָה

Match each phrase with a correct picture.

תּוֹרָה עִם רִמּוֹנִים

תּוֹרָה שֶׁל אַשְׁכְּנַזִּים עִם מְעִיל

תּוֹרָה עִם יָד

תּוֹרָה שֶׁל סְפָרַדִּים עִם תִּיק

חֹשֶׁן בְּלִי תּוֹרָה

תּוֹרָה בְּלִי אַבְנֵט

Yidbit: The Fish and the Fox

KEY WORDS:

תּוֹרָה וּמִצְוֹת

There is a very famous story in the Talmud that explains how important Torah is to the Jewish people.

During the time of Rabbi Akiva, the Roman government forbade the Jews to study or practice Torah. A Jewish man named Pappas ben Judah saw Rabbi Akiva teaching Torah in public. He asked the Rabbi, "Akiva, aren't you afraid of the government?" Rabbi Akiva answered him with this fable:

A fox was once walking along the bank of a river. He saw fish swimming frantically back and forth. The fox asked them, "From what are you fleeing?" The fish answered, "From the fishermen's nets." The fox said, "Wouldn't you like to come up to the dry land, so that you and I could live together just like our ancestors used to?" The fish replied, "You think you're so clever! You're not clever, you're a fool! If we are afraid in the water, which gives us our life, imagine how much more afraid we would be on the land, where we would surely die."

Akiva continued, "It's the same with us. If things are hard for us when we are sitting and studying Torah (of which it is written, *For it is your life and the length of your days'*), imagine how much worse off we'd be if we ignored the Torah." *(Talmud, Berachot 61b)*

1. Akiva tells a fable to explain himself. In a fable, animals and objects symbolize other things. In this fable . . .

   fish = _____

   fishermen and their nets = _____

   water = _____

   dry land = _____

2. Rabbi Akiva quotes the Torah to support his opinion.

   כִּי הוּא חַיֶּיךָ וְאֹרֶךְ יָמֶיךָ
   דְּבָרִים ל׳ כ׳

   "For it is your life and the length of your days."
   (Deuteronomy 30:20)

Find the five-word phrase in the אַהֲבַת עוֹלָם prayer that is very similar to the biblical quote Rabbi Akiva used. (You can find it on page 46.)

_____ _____ _____ _____ _____

CHAPTER **5**

TEXT EXploration

תּוֹרָה וּמִצְוֹת, חֻקִּים וּמִשְׁפָּטִים אוֹתָנוּ לִמַּדְתָּ.

Torah and Mitzvot, laws and judgments You have taught us.

The Rabbis had many ways of classifying the 613 מִצְוֹת. They said the מִשְׁפָּטִים were commandments that had reasons given for them, such as:

Be kind to people who are different from you, because you were a stranger in Egypt.

They called the commandments that have no reason given for them חֻקִּים.
For example: **Do not eat pork.**

Here is another way the Rabbis classified מִצְוֹת:

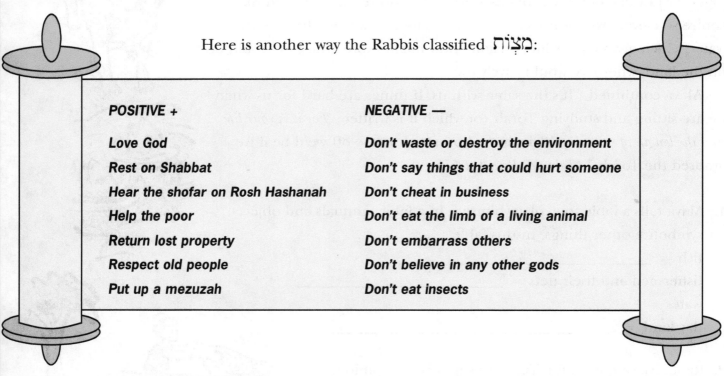

POSITIVE +	NEGATIVE —
Love God	Don't waste or destroy the environment
Rest on Shabbat	Don't say things that could hurt someone
Hear the shofar on Rosh Hashanah	Don't cheat in business
Help the poor	Don't eat the limb of a living animal
Return lost property	Don't embarrass others
Respect old people	Don't believe in any other gods
Put up a mezuzah	Don't eat insects

1. The Rabbis noticed that many מִצְוֹת could only be done at a certain time.
   Draw a clock next to two מִצְוֹת like that.

2. Some מִצְוֹת have to do with relationships between people, others are about people's relationship with God. Write a **P** next to the people-to-people מִצְוֹת.

3. What kinds of categories could you make for the מִצְוֹת on the lists?
   My Categories

   _____ and _____

   _____ and _____

מִצְוֹת: The Path to a Good Life

How can an ordinary person turn into a truly good person? The Rabbis taught that most of us cannot go from being a "sinner" to being a "saint" in one step. Instead, they suggested we choose one mitzvah, and start doing it. Once doing that first mitzvah becomes a habit, then we can choose another mitzvah, and focus on it.

On page 52, you looked at a number of mitzvot from the Torah. Select one mitzvah that you would like to work on this year. It can be a positive or a negative mitzvah, or one from any other category. You can choose a mitzvah from the list on page 52, or you can select any other one that you feel strongly about.

My מִצְוָה goal: _____

Think about the mitzvah you chose as you recite the אַהֲבַת עוֹלָם prayer quietly to yourself.

אַהֲבַת עוֹלָם בֵּית יִשְׂרָאֵל עַמְּךָ אָהָבְתָּ. תּוֹרָה וּמִצְוֹת, חֻקִּים
וּמִשְׁפָּטִים אוֹתָנוּ לִמַּדְתָּ. עַל־כֵּן, יְיָ אֱלֹהֵינוּ, בְּשָׁכְבֵנוּ
וּבְקוּמֵנוּ נָשִׂיחַ בְּחֻקֶּיךָ, וְנִשְׂמַח בְּדִבְרֵי תוֹרָתֶךָ וּבְמִצְוֹתֶיךָ
לְעוֹלָם וָעֶד. כִּי הֵם חַיֵּינוּ וְאֹרֶךְ יָמֵינוּ, וּבָהֶם נֶהְגֶּה
יוֹמָם וָלָיְלָה. וְאַהֲבָתְךָ אַל־תָּסִיר מִמֶּנּוּ לְעוֹלָמִים!
בָּרוּךְ אַתָּה יְיָ, אוֹהֵב עַמּוֹ יִשְׂרָאֵל.

Now that you've learned about the important rules found in the Torah, it's time to continue your journey, and to discover the importance of studying the Torah.

The Steps to Wisdom

KEY WORDS:
תַּלְמוּד תּוֹרָה

**In acquiring wisdom, the first step is silence,
the second is listening, the third is
remembering, the fourth is practicing,
and the fifth — teaching others.**

(Solomon ibn Gabirol, 11th Century Spanish Hebrew Poet)

In our tradition, study and teaching are like two sides of a single coin. We call this idea תַּלְמוּד תּוֹרָה. We find the steps involved in תַּלְמוּד תּוֹרָה listed in the אַהֲבָה רַבָּה prayer.

Climb the steps of learning. Take turns reading these words with a partner. If you make a mistake, you lose your turn, and must begin again at the bottom of the steps. Keep reading until both of you can climb the steps without a mistake.

to practice	לְקַיֵּם
to do	לַעֲשׂוֹת
to observe	לִשְׁמֹר
to teach	לְלַמֵּד
to learn	לִלְמֹד
to hear	לִשְׁמֹעַ
to grow wise	לְהַשְׂכִּיל
to understand	לְהָבִין

Isaac's Teacher

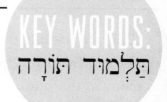

תַּלְמוּד תּוֹרָה

"Okay, kids," Mrs. Shapiro said as the bell rang, "don't forget your homework assignments. I'll see you next week."

As the class began to spill into the hall, Mrs. Shapiro asked Michael to stay for a moment. "How would you like to do a major mitzvah?"

"Uh, I guess so," Michael answered.

"A new boy is joining our class next week. His name is Isaac Klein."

"I know him! He's on my soccer team."

"Great. Then maybe you'd be willing to help him out. He's going to be behind the rest of the class, and I was wondering if you'd be willing to work with him a little until he catches up."

Michael shrugged his shoulders. "I don't know," he said. "I'm not a teacher or anything."

Mrs. Shapiro smiled. "Don't sell yourself short. I've been watching you all year, and I think you're a born teacher. You have a real gift for explaining the ideas we've been discussing in class."

"But that's not really teaching."

"Sure it is. You explain, your study partner listens and understands. She explains and you understand."

"And that's teaching?"

"That's it exactly. You've been teaching all along and you didn't even realize it!"

Michael's Lesson Plan

At their first meeting, Michael showed Isaac the prayers that the class had been studying. He made a list for Michael to study:

Morning		Evening	
page 22	בָּרְכוּ	page 22	בָּרְכוּ
page 36	יוֹצֵר אוֹר	page 25	מַעֲרִיב עֲרָבִים
page 57	אַהֲבָה רַבָּה	page 46	אַהֲבַת עוֹלָם

Review the prayers that you have studied so far.

Speed Reading

Practice reading these phrases with a partner until both of you can read them fluently. Then have your partner time you while you read. Read as many of the phrases as you can in one minute. If you make a mistake, your partner should say, "Try again." Write down the number of phrases you read correctly. Try again, and see if you can beat your old score.

א. אֶת־כָּל־דִּבְרֵי תַּלְמוּד תּוֹרָתֶךָ בְּאַהֲבָה   אֶת־כָּל־דִּבְרֵי תַּלְמוּד תּוֹרָתֶךָ בְּאַהֲבָה

ב. וְהָאֵר עֵינֵינוּ בְּתוֹרָתֶךָ   וְהָאֵר עֵינֵינוּ בְּתוֹרָתֶךָ

ג. וְדַבֵּק לִבֵּנוּ בְּמִצְוֹתֶיךָ   וְדַבֵּק לִבֵּנוּ בְּמִצְוֹתֶיךָ

ד. לְאַהֲבָה וּלְיִרְאָה אֶת־שְׁמֶךָ   לְאַהֲבָה וּלְיִרְאָה אֶת־שְׁמֶךָ

ה. כִּי בְשֵׁם קָדְשְׁךָ   כִּי בְשֵׁם קָדְשְׁךָ

ו. וְקֵרַבְתָּנוּ לְשִׁמְךָ הַגָּדוֹל סֶלָה בֶּאֱמֶת   וְקֵרַבְתָּנוּ לְשִׁמְךָ הַגָּדוֹל סֶלָה בֶּאֱמֶת

ז. לְהוֹדוֹת לְךָ וּלְיַחֶדְךָ בְּאַהֲבָה   לְהוֹדוֹת לְךָ וּלְיַחֶדְךָ בְּאַהֲבָה

My Scores: 1st Try _____ 2nd Try _____ 3rd Try _____ 4th Try _____

Circle the Word

Read each phrase and circle the word indicated.

1. Circle the word that contains the key word meaning "name".   כִּי בְשֵׁם קָדְשְׁךָ

2. Circle the word that contains תּוֹרָה.   וְהָאֵר עֵינֵינוּ בְּתוֹרָתֶךָ

3. Circle the word that contains מִצְוֹת.   וְדַבֵּק לִבֵּנוּ בְּמִצְוֹתֶיךָ

4. Circle the word that contains the word שֵׁם.   לְאַהֲבָה וּלְיִרְאָה אֶת־שְׁמֶךָ

5. Circle all the words that end with the same letter.   לְהוֹדוֹת לְךָ וּלְיַחֶדְךָ בְּאַהֲבָה

6. Circle the antonym of הַקָּטָן.   וְקֵרַבְתָּנוּ לְשִׁמְךָ הַגָּדוֹל סֶלָה בֶּאֱמֶת

7. Circle the words that contain the Key Words from this chapter.   אֶת־כָּל־דִּבְרֵי תַּלְמוּד תּוֹרָתֶךָ בְּאַהֲבָה.

אַהֲבָה רַבָּה

Great is Your love for us, Adonai our God,	1. אַהֲבָה רַבָּה אֲהַבְתָּנוּ, יְיָ אֱלֹהֵינוּ,
Abundant is Your compassion for us.	2. חֶמְלָה גְדוֹלָה וִיתֵרָה חָמַלְתָּ עָלֵינוּ.
Our Maker and Ruler, for the sake of	3. אָבִינוּ מַלְכֵּנוּ, בַּעֲבוּר אֲבוֹתֵינוּ
our ancestors who trusted in You	4. שֶׁבָּטְחוּ בְךָ
and whom You did teach the laws of life,	5. וַתְּלַמְּדֵם חֻקֵּי חַיִּים,
be gracious to us and teach us.	6. כֵּן תְּחָנֵּנוּ וּתְלַמְּדֵנוּ.
Source of Mercy,	7. אָבִינוּ הָאָב הָרַחֲמָן,
have compassion on us	8. הַמְרַחֵם, רַחֵם עָלֵינוּ
and place in our hearts the ability to	9. וְתֵן בְּלִבֵּנוּ לְהָבִין וּלְהַשְׂכִּיל,
understand and grow wise, to hear, to learn	10. לִשְׁמֹעַ, לִלְמֹד וּלְלַמֵּד,
and to teach, to observe, to do, and to practice all the	11. לִשְׁמֹר וְלַעֲשׂוֹת וּלְקַיֵּם
teachings of Your Torah with love.	12. אֶת-כָּל-דִּבְרֵי תַלְמוּד תּוֹרָתֶךָ בְּאַהֲבָה.
Enlighten our eyes with Your Torah,	13. וְהָאֵר עֵינֵינוּ בְּתוֹרָתֶךָ,
and make our hearts cling to Your mitzvot,	14. וְדַבֵּק לִבֵּנוּ בְּמִצְוֹתֶיךָ,
and unite our hearts	15. וְיַחֵד לְבָבֵנוּ
to love and respect Your Name.	16. לְאַהֲבָה וּלְיִרְאָה אֶת-שְׁמֶךָ
Then we will never be shamed.	17. וְלֹא-נֵבוֹשׁ לְעוֹלָם וָעֶד.
For we put our trust in Your holy,	18. כִּי בְשֵׁם קָדְשְׁךָ
great, and awesome Name,	20. הַגָּדוֹל וְהַנּוֹרָא בָּטָחְנוּ,
we will rejoice and be glad for Your rescue.	21. נָגִילָה וְנִשְׂמְחָה בִּישׁוּעָתֶךָ.
* Gather us in peace from	וַהֲבִיאֵנוּ לְשָׁלוֹם
the four corners of the earth,	מֵאַרְבַּע כַּנְפוֹת הָאָרֶץ,
and bring us with dignity to our land,	וְתוֹלִיכֵנוּ קוֹמְמִיּוּת לְאַרְצֵנוּ,
For You, O God, work miraculous rescues,	22. כִּי אֵל פּוֹעֵל יְשׁוּעוֹת אָתָּה,
and You chose us from all peoples,	23. וּבָנוּ בָחַרְתָּ מִכָּל-עַם וְלָשׁוֹן,
and drew us near Your great Name,	24. וְקֵרַבְתָּנוּ לְשִׁמְךָ הַגָּדוֹל סֶלָה בֶּאֱמֶת,
to thank You and lovingly proclaim Your unity.	25. לְהוֹדוֹת לְךָ וּלְיַחֶדְךָ בְּאַהֲבָה.
Blessed are You, Adonai,	26. בָּרוּךְ אַתָּה יְיָ
Who has chosen Your people Israel with love.	27. הַבּוֹחֵר בְּעַמּוֹ יִשְׂרָאֵל בְּאַהֲבָה.

* The shaded phrases are omitted in Liberal congregations.

The Twelve Gates

The Traditional version of אַהֲבָה רַבָּה has one line that is not found in the Liberal version. This line asks God to bring all Jews to live in the Land of Israel. It is a mitzvah to live in the Land of Israel. However, Liberal Jews believe that certain mitzvot are a matter of personal choice. These include keeping kosher, wearing a tallit, and living in Israel. They believe that each individual must think about the reasons for these mitzvot and then decide what he or she should do.

Read both columns below and check those reasons in each category with which you agree.

Reasons for living in Israel

❑ Israel is the land that was given to Abraham, Isaac, and Jacob. It was promised to the Jewish people forever.

❑ It's a mitzvah to live in Israel.

❑ If all Jews lived together, Israel would be a great and powerful nation.

❑ Jews are not a minority in Israel. You would never have to explain why your customs are different.

❑ Israel is the only country that has vowed to protect the Jewish people from anti-Semitic acts such as the Holocaust.

❑ Israel is the only Jewish country in the world. Shabbat, national holidays, and all Jewish festivals are observed there. It is the only place on earth where one can live a fully Jewish life.

Reasons for living outside Israel

❑ Israel needs the support of countries around the world. Jews who live outside of Israel can help to provide that support.

❑ It can be dangerous to live in Israel.

❑ As free people, we should have the right to decide for ourselves where we want to live.

❑ It would be very difficult to move to a foreign country, leaving familiar people and places behind.

❑ Diversity is one of our greatest strengths as a people. Much of our diversity comes from the many places we have called home.

❑ Our tradition teaches that Jews are "a light to the nations"— that we are supposed to teach others about the One God. This is best done by living in many different places.

**The Bible, the Land of Israel, and the Hebrew language
are the Jewish people's most precious possessions.
Turn the page to see how these are all connected.**

Yidbit

Hebrew is one of the oldest languages in the world. It is also the newest. Hebrew was first spoken in the days of the Bible. When the Jewish people were scattered around the world, they began to speak other languages. However, they continued to use Hebrew for prayer and study.

In the 1800s, Jews began to resettle the Land of Israel. The only language they shared was Hebrew. The problem was that ancient Hebrew did not have words for many of the things found in the modern world.

Think of all the things that have been invented since the time of the Bible. List four of these things:

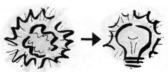

_____ _____

_____ _____

In 1881, a medical student named Eliezer Ben Yehuda formed the Hebrew Language Committee. Its members included writers and poets as well as experts in Hebrew, Arabic, and other languages. One method the Committee used to modernize Hebrew was to assign new meanings to ancient Hebrew words.

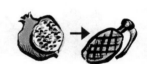

MODERN MEANING	BIBLICAL MEANING	
electricity	shining substance	חַשְׁמַל
president	prince or chief	נָשִׂיא
hand grenade	pomegranate	רִמּוֹן
train	(רֶכֶב) chariot	רַכֶּבֶת
computer	(חָשַׁב) think	מַחְשֵׁב

In the prayer **אַהֲבָה רַבָּה** we find the phrase:

וְדַבֵּק לִבֵּנוּ בְּמִצְוֹתֶיךָ

(". . . make our hearts cling to Your Commandments . . .")

The ancient verb דָּבַק (cling) has come into modern Hebrew as דֶּבֶק (glue). What is the connection between clinging and glue?

Modernizing ancient words is one way of creating new Hebrew words. On the next page you can explore the most important way that new Hebrew words are formed.

Language Enrichment

אוֹצַר מִלִּים
A TREASURY OF WORDS

The Root of the Matter

In Hebrew, many words can grow from a single root.
Study each of these words and answer the questions.

שׁוֹמֵעַ

שׁוֹמַעַת

שְׁמַע!

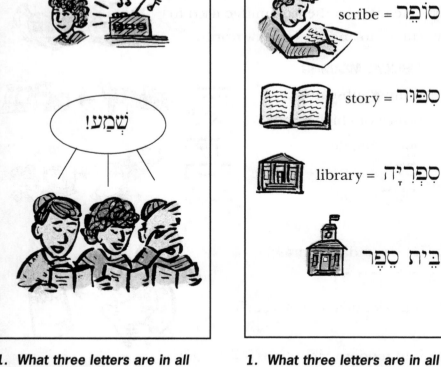

סֵפֶר

סֵפֶר תּוֹרָה

scribe = סוֹפֵר

story = סִפּוּר

library = סִפְרִיָּה

בֵּית סֵפֶר

לוֹמֵד

לוֹמֶדֶת

מְלַמֵּד

מְלַמֶּדֶת

תַּלְמוּד

תַּלְמוּד תּוֹרָה

---

1. What three letters are in all these words? ____ ____ ____

2. All of the words in this column are related. What basic meaning do they all share?

_____

1. What three letters are in all these words? ____ ____ ____

2. All of the words in this column are related. What basic meaning do they all share?

_____

1. What three letters are in all these words? ____ ____ ____

2. All of the words in this column are related. What basic meaning do they all share?

_____

The Root of the Matter

Fill in the missing words for each word family tree. Remember: each member of these word families shares the same three root letters as the other members of the family. An example has been done for you in each tree.

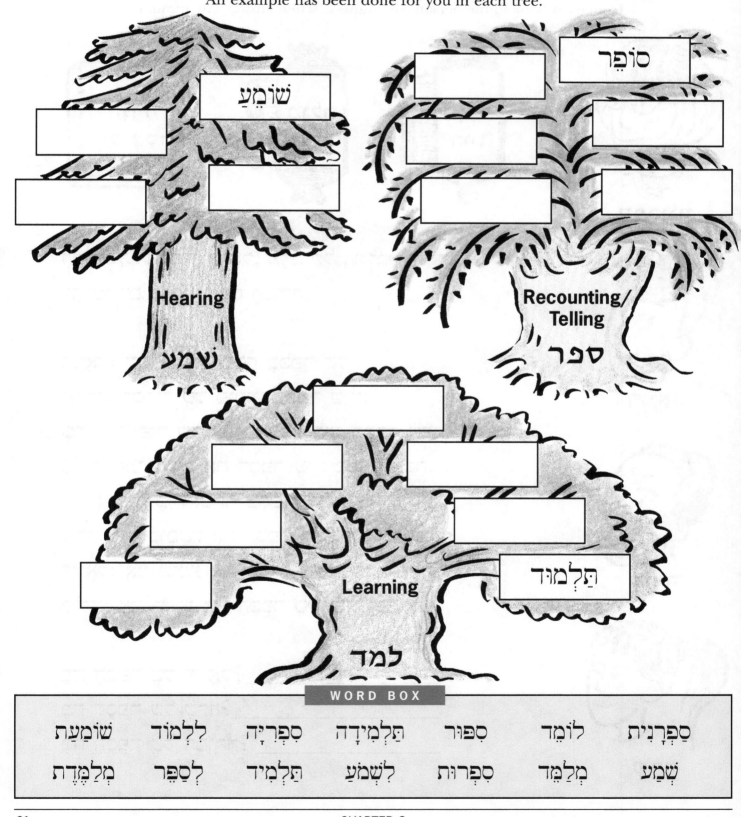

שׁוֹמֵעַ

Hearing

שמע

סוֹפֵר

Recounting/
Telling

ספר

תַּלְמוּד

Learning

למד

WORD BOX

שׁוֹמַעַת	לִלְמוֹד	סִפְרִיָּה	תַּלְמִידָה	סִפּוּר	לוֹמֵד	סַפְרָנִית
מְלַמֶּדֶת	לְסַפֵּר	תַּלְמִיד	לִשְׁמֹעַ	סְפָרוֹת	מְלַמֵּד	שָׁמַע

בַּסִפְרִיָּה

Help the librarian find the correct book for each person. Draw a line
from each book to the person who wants it. Then answer the questions.

סִפְרָנִית

דָּנִיאֵל

הַשֵּׁם שֶׁל הַתַּלְמִיד דָּנִיאֵל. הַשֵּׁם שֶׁל הַתַּלְמִידָה שָׂרָה.
הַתַּלְמִידִים בַּסִפְרִיָּה עִם הַמּוֹרֶה.

דָּנִיאֵל: הַסִפּוּר שֶׁל פֶּסַח בַּסֵּפֶר שֶׁלִי.
מוֹרֶה: הַסִפּוּר שֶׁל פּוּרִים בַּסֵּפֶר שֶׁלִי.
שָׂרָה: הַסִפּוּר שֶׁל רוּת, נָעֳמִי, וּבֹעַז בַּסֵּפֶר שֶׁלִי.
מוֹרֶה: אֲנִי שׁוֹמֵעַ אֶת הַסֵּפֶר שֶׁלִי בְּבֵית כְּנֶסֶת.
מָרְדְּכַי וְאֶסְתֵּר בַּסֵּפֶר שֶׁלִי.
שָׂרָה: אֲנִי שׁוֹמַעַת אֶת הַסֵּפֶר שֶׁלִי בְּחַג שָׁבוּעוֹת.
דָּנִיאֵל: אֲנִי שׁוֹמֵעַ אֶת הַסֵּפֶר שֶׁלִי בְּסֵדֶר פֶּסַח.
מוֹרֶה: אֲנִי שׁוֹמֵעַ אֶת הַסֵּפֶר שֶׁלִי בְּחַג פּוּרִים.

מוֹרֶה

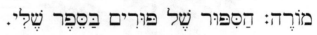

מַה הַסֵּפֶר שֶׁל דָּנִיאֵל? _____
מַה הַסֵּפֶר שֶׁל שָׂרָה? _____
מַה הַסֵּפֶר שֶׁל הַמּוֹרֶה? _____

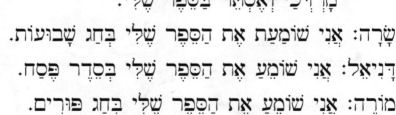

שָׂרָה

The People of the Book and the Book of the People

The Jewish People are often called עַם הַסֵּפֶר ("the People of the Book"). This nickname tells us how important the Torah has always been to our people, as well as how much we value all kinds of books and learning.

Imagine that it is your Bar or Bat Mitzvah, and you are reading from the Torah, our most holy book. Now recite the אַהֲבָה רַבָּה prayer quietly to yourself.

אַהֲבָה רַבָּה אֲהַבְתָּנוּ, יְיָ אֱלֹהֵינוּ, חֶמְלָה גְדוֹלָה וִיתֵרָה חָמַלְתָּ
עָלֵינוּ. אָבִינוּ מַלְכֵּנוּ, בַּעֲבוּר אֲבוֹתֵינוּ שֶׁבָּטְחוּ בְךָ וַתְּלַמְּדֵם
חֻקֵּי חַיִּים, כֵּן תְּחָנֵּנוּ וּתְלַמְּדֵנוּ. אָבִינוּ הָאָב הָרַחֲמָן, הַמְרַחֵם,
רַחֵם עָלֵינוּ. וְתֵן בְּלִבֵּנוּ לְהָבִין וּלְהַשְׂכִּיל, לִשְׁמֹעַ, לִלְמֹד וּלְלַמֵּד,
לִשְׁמֹר וְלַעֲשׂוֹת וּלְקַיֵּם אֶת־כָּל־דִּבְרֵי תַלְמוּד תּוֹרָתֶךָ בְּאַהֲבָה.
וְהָאֵר עֵינֵינוּ בְּתוֹרָתֶךָ, וְדַבֵּק לִבֵּנוּ בְּמִצְוֹתֶיךָ, וְיַחֵד לְבָבֵנוּ
לְאַהֲבָה וּלְיִרְאָה אֶת־שְׁמֶךָ. וְלֹא נֵבוֹשׁ לְעוֹלָם וָעֶד.
כִּי בְשֵׁם קָדְשְׁךָ הַגָּדוֹל וְהַנּוֹרָא בָּטָחְנוּ, נָגִילָה וְנִשְׂמְחָה בִּישׁוּעָתֶךָ.

וַהֲבִיאֵנוּ לְשָׁלוֹם מֵאַרְבַּע כַּנְפוֹת הָאָרֶץ, וְתוֹלִיכֵנוּ
קוֹמְמִיּוּת לְאַרְצֵנוּ,

כִּי אֵל פּוֹעֵל יְשׁוּעוֹת אָתָּה, וּבָנוּ בָחַרְתָּ מִכָּל־עַם וְלָשׁוֹן,

וְקֵרַבְתָּנוּ לְשִׁמְךָ הַגָּדוֹל סֶלָה בֶּאֱמֶת, לְהוֹדוֹת לְךָ וּלְיַחֶדְךָ
בְּאַהֲבָה. בָּרוּךְ אַתָּה יְיָ, הַבּוֹחֵר בְּעַמּוֹ יִשְׂרָאֵל בְּאַהֲבָה.

= Omitted in Liberal congregations.

Like אַהֲבָה רַבָּה, which is recited at night, אַהֲבַת עוֹלָם reminds us that the Torah is our "tree of life". Its laws provide a guide for living a life filled with goodness. Its words are full of wisdom. Now that you know how special the Torah is, it's time to learn its most important passage (which also happens to be the Jewish people's most important prayer).

שְׁמַע

KEY WORD:
אֶחָד

Leader and Congregation one time:
שְׁמַע יִשְׂרָאֵל יְיָ אֱלֹהֵינוּ, יְיָ אֶחָד.

Leader and Congregation three times:
בָּרוּךְ שֵׁם כְּבוֹד מַלְכוּתוֹ לְעוֹלָם וָעֶד.

Leader and Congregation seven times:
יְיָ הוּא הָאֱלֹהִים.

Sounding the Shofar:
תְּקִיעָה גְדוֹלָה

לְשָׁנָה הַבָּאָה בִּירוּשָׁלָיִם.

אֵל מֶלֶךְ נֶאֱמָן
שְׁמַע יִשְׂרָאֵל יְיָ אֱלֹהֵינוּ, יְיָ אֶחָד.
בָּרוּךְ שֵׁם כְּבוֹד מַלְכוּתוֹ לְעוֹלָם וָעֶד.

שְׁמַע יִשְׂרָאֵל יְיָ אֱלֹהֵינוּ, יְיָ אֶחָד.
אֶחָד אֱלֹהֵינוּ, גָּדוֹל אֲדוֹנֵינוּ, קָדוֹשׁ שְׁמוֹ.

Hear O Israel:

Adonai is our God, Adonai is One.

*Blessed is God's name

Honored is God's sovereignty forever.

שְׁמַע יִשְׂרָאֵל:
יְיָ אֱלֹהֵינוּ, יְיָ אֶחָד.
בָּרוּךְ שֵׁם
כְּבוֹד מַלְכוּתוֹ לְעוֹלָם וָעֶד.

These two lines are said silently in some congregations.

The שְׁמַע is the most important Jewish prayer. According to our tradition, when you recite the שְׁמַע, you should close or cover your eyes to help you concentrate on the meaning of each word.

Yidbit

From Israel's birth in 1948 until 1967, Jerusalem was a divided city. The eastern part of Jerusalem, including the Old City, was under the control of Jordan. During that time, Jews were not allowed to pray at the Western Wall, the holiest site for the Jewish people.

Early in June of 1967, Israel's Arab neighbors declared war on the Jewish State. On June 6th, Israel's forces recaptured East Jerusalem. The next day, Israeli troops burst into the Old City, and soon reclaimed the area around the ancient Temple Mount, including the Western Wall.

General Moshe Dayan, one of Israel's greatest military leaders, was then the Minister of Defense. Soon after Jerusalem was reunited, Moshe Dayan made an inspection of the Old City, stopping at the Western Wall. There, General Dayan followed the tradition of writing a prayer on a small piece of paper and placing it between the stones of the Wall.

CRACK THE CODE!

In Hebrew, every letter also has a number value. Study the number value for each letter.

ט	ח	ז	ו	ה	ד	ג	ב/בּ	א
9	8	7	6	5	4	3	2	1

צ/ץ	פ/פּ/ף	ע	ס	נ/ן	מ/ם	ל	כ/כּ/ךּ	י
90	80	70	60	50	40	30	20	10

ת/תּ	שׁ/שׂ	ר	ק
400	300	200	100

**Help Israeli Intelligence crack the code to discover General Dayan's message.
Write the Hebrew letter for each number onto the line below.
(Use final letters at the end of words.)**

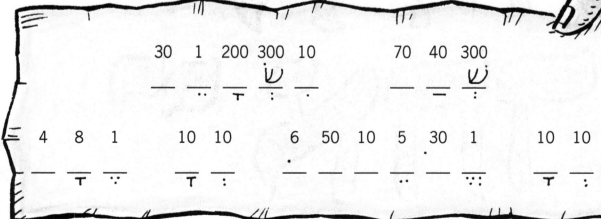

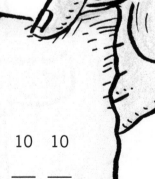

30 1 200 300 10   70 40 300

4 8 1   10 10   6 50 10 5 30 1   10 10

TEXT EXploration

Even though it is very short, the שְׁמַע is one of the most meaningful prayers. Each word is rich with associations. Find a partner and study the words in each Hebrew word outline. Then circle the words that are most meaningful for you. Add your own ideas around the Hebrew words.

The Secret of שׁ.מ.ע.

According to Abudarham, the fourteenth century Spanish commentator, the word שְׁמַע is an acronym (a word made from the first letters of other words) and can stand for many different things:

1. The morning, afternoon, and evening prayer services

שַׁחֲרִית

מִנְחָה

עַרְבִית

2. "Lift up your eyes to the heavens."

שְׂאוּ

מָרוֹם

עֵינֵיכֶם

3. "God is the highest Ruler."

שַׁדַּי

מֶלֶךְ

עֶלְיוֹן

Write an acronym of your own for the word שְׁמַע in Hebrew or English.
(You may use your Dictionary.)

S _____   _____ שׁ

H _____   _____ מ

E _____   _____ ע

M _____

A _____

Language Enrichment

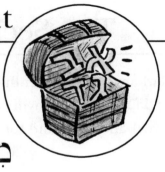

אוֹצַר מִלִּים
A TREASURY OF WORDS

מִסְפָּרִים

תֵּשַׁע	חָמֵשׁ	אַחַת
עֶשֶׂר	שֵׁשׁ	שְׁתַּיִם
אֶפֶס	שֶׁבַע	שָׁלוֹשׁ
שְׁמוֹנֶה		אַרְבַּע

מַה מִסְפַּר הַטֶּלֶפוֹן? = What's the phone number?

In the spaces below, write your name and phone number. Then, exchange phone numbers in Hebrew with five other students in your class.

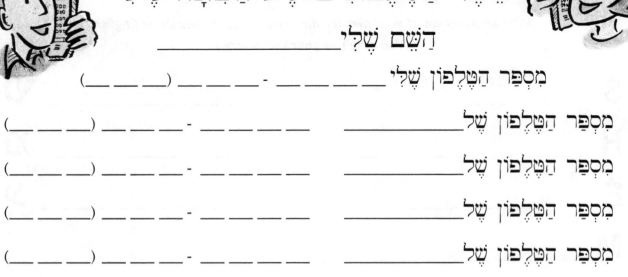

סֵפֶר הַטֶּלֶפוֹנִים שֶׁל הַכִּתָּה שֶׁלִי

הַשֵׁם שֶׁלִי _____

מִסְפַּר הַטֶּלֶפוֹן שֶׁלִי _____ _____ - _____ (_____)

מִסְפַּר הַטֶּלֶפוֹן שֶׁל _____ _____ _____ - _____ (_____)

מִסְפַּר הַטֶּלֶפוֹן שֶׁל _____ _____ _____ - _____ (_____)

מִסְפַּר הַטֶּלֶפוֹן שֶׁל _____ _____ _____ - _____ (_____)

מִסְפַּר הַטֶּלֶפוֹן שֶׁל _____ _____ _____ - _____ (_____)

מִסְפַּר הַטֶּלֶפוֹן שֶׁל _____ _____ _____ - _____ (_____)

Language Enrichment

How many? = ‏כַּמָּה?‏
‏שְׁתַּיִם / שְׁתֵּי‏

Read the Hebrew captions and draw in the missing parts of each picture.
Then answer the questions that follow.

‏יֵשׁ לָרַבִּי שְׁתֵּי כִּפּוֹת.‏

‏יֵשׁ לְרִבְקָה סֵפֶר אֶחָד.‏

‏יֵשׁ לְיוֹסִי חָמֵשׁ מַחְבָּרוֹת.‏

‏יֵשׁ שָׁלוֹשׁ מַצּוֹת עַל הַשֻּׁלְחָן בְּסֵדֶר פֶּסַח.‏

‏יֵשׁ שְׁתֵּי חֲתוּלוֹת וְכֶלֶב אֶחָד עַל־יַד הַבַּיִת שֶׁל מִיכָאֵל.‏

1. ‏כַּמָּה כּוֹסוֹת יַיִן יֵשׁ עַל הַשֻּׁלְחָן בְּסֵדֶר פֶּסַח?‏ _____

2. ‏כַּמָּה טַלִּיתוֹת יֵשׁ לָרַבִּי?‏ _____

3. ‏כַּמָּה יְלָדוֹת יֵשׁ עַל־יַד הַבַּיִת שֶׁל מִיכָאֵל?‏ _____

1. What is your favorite, or "lucky," number? Write it in Hebrew. _____

2. In your opinion, what is the most important number? _____

Why? _____

Prayerobics

The שְׁמַע is the most important Jewish prayer. According to our tradition, when reciting the שְׁמַע, some people close their eyes, while others cover their eyes with their hand. This is to help us focus on the meaning of each and every word. At the end of the אַהֲבָה רַבָּה prayer, those who wear a טַלִית during morning services gather the four צִיצִת together. Then they cover their eyes with the צִיצִת when reciting the שְׁמַע.

Try this experiment:
Recite the שְׁמַע in each of these four ways:
- With your eyes open.
- With your eyes closed.
- With your eyes covered by your hand.
- With your eyes covered by the צִיצִת of your טַלִית.

According to a midrash, when Moses brought the Ten Commandments down from Mount Sinai, the entire Jewish people, including those who had died and those who had not yet been born, gathered at the foot of the mountain to witness this event. That is why the שְׁמַע is written in the Torah with two larger letters.

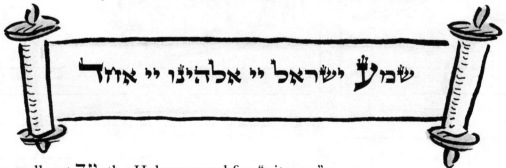

שמע ישראל יי אלהינו יי אחד

These two letters spell out עֵד, the Hebrew word for "witness."

Be a witness. Close your eyes, and imagine that you are standing at the foot of Mount Sinai while Moses is bringing the Ten Commandments down. Keep this image in your mind as you recite the שְׁמַע quietly to yourself.

The blessing just before the שְׁמַע reminds us that God loves us, and cares about us. Through the paragraph that follows the שְׁמַע, we learn how to show our love for God.

וְאָהַבְתָּ

דַּף קְרִיאָה
READING PAGE

KEY WORD:
אַהֲבָה

READING REMINDER

In the following words, the ▯ followed by a ▯
is pronounced "oh." Practice reading these words.

וּבְשָׁכְבְּךָ   קָדְשֶׁךָ   קָדְשׁוֹ   זָכְרֵנוּ

SUPER READING SECRET

Inside a word the ▯ is usually silent. But in the following words, the ▯
in the second letter is pronounced "e" as in bed:

וּבְכָל = וּ + בְּכָל   הַדְּבָרִים = הַ + דְּבָ + רִים

Practice reading these words.

וּבְשָׁכְבְּךָ	בְּשָׁכְבְּךָ	וּבְקוּמֶךָ	בְּקוּמֶךָ	הַדְּבָרִים	דְּבָרִים	א.
וּבְשְׁעָרֶיךָ	בִּשְׁעָרֶיךָ	וּבְלֶכְתְּךָ	בְּלֶכְתְּךָ	וּקְשַׁרְתָּם	קְשַׁרְתָּם	ב.
		וּבְכָל-נַפְשְׁךָ	בְּכָל	וּבְכָל-מְאֹדֶךָ	בְּכָל	ג.

The prefix וֹ means "and." The prefix _____ means "the."

Many words appear in different forms. Practice reading these words in all of their forms.

וְאָהַבְתָּ	אָהַבְתָּ	אַהֲבָה	וְאָהַב	אָהַב	1.
בְּבֵיתֶךָ	בֵּיתֶךָ	בַּיִת	יָדֶךָ	יָד	2.
לְבָבֶךָ	לְבָבְךָ	לֵב	עֵינֶיךָ	עַיִן	3.
נַפְשְׁךָ	נֶפֶשׁ	לְבָנֶיךָ	בָּנֶיךָ	בֵּן	4.
מְאֹדֶךָ	מְאֹד	וְדִבַּרְתָּ	הַדְּבָרִים	דָּבָר	5.
וּבִשְׁעָרֶיךָ	בִּשְׁעָרֶיךָ	שְׁעָרֶיךָ	שְׁעָרִים	שַׁעַר	6.

Now practice reading the words found inside every מְזוּזָה.

וּכְתַבְתָּם עַל־מְזֻזוֹת בֵּיתֶךָ

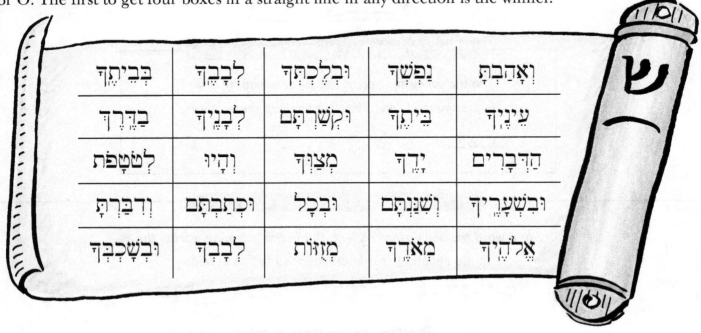

Twice every seven years, the parchment inside a מְזוּזָה must be inspected to make sure that the writing is still clear enough to read. Check this מְזוּזָה parchment with a partner. One of you is X, the other is O. Take turns reading the Hebrew words in any box below. If you read correctly, mark the box with your X or O. The first to get four boxes in a straight line in any direction is the winner.

KEY WORD: אַהֲבָה

בְּבֵיתֶךָ	לְבָבֶךָ	וּבְלֶכְתְּךָ	נַפְשֶׁךָ	וְאָהַבְתָּ
בַּדֶּרֶךְ	לְבָנֶיךָ	וּקְשַׁרְתָּם	בֵּיתֶךָ	עֵינֶיךָ
לְטֹטָפֹת	וְהָיוּ	מְצַוְּךָ	יָדֶךָ	הַדְּבָרִים
וְדִבַּרְתָּ	וּכְתַבְתָּם	וּבְכָל	וְשִׁנַּנְתָּם	וּבִשְׁעָרֶיךָ
וּבְשָׁכְבְּךָ	לְבָבֶךָ	מְזֻזוֹת	מְאֹדֶךָ	אֱלֹהֶיךָ

Write each word in its proper word family box. An example has been done for you.

לוֹמֵד ✓	אוֹהֵב	בָּרוּךְ	לוֹמֶדֶת	אֲהוּבִים
תַּלְמוּד	בְּרָכוֹת	אוֹהֶבֶת	הַמְבֹרָךְ	לִמּוּדֵי
בָּרְכוּ	וְאָהַבְתָּ	בְּרָכָה	וְתִלַּמְדֶם	אַהֲבָה

אהב

_____
_____
_____

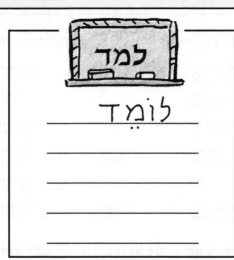

למד

לוֹמֵד
_____
_____

ברך

_____
_____
_____

וּבְשָׁכְבְּךָ וּבְקוּמֶךָ
And When You Lie Down and When You Rise Up

Practice reading these phrases. Then answer the questions.

א. וְשִׁנַּנְתָּם לְבָנֶיךָ

ב. בֵּיתֶךָ וּבִשְׁעָרֶיךָ

ו. וּכְתַבְתָּם עַל-מְזוּזוֹת

י. וְהָיוּ הַדְּבָרִים הָאֵלֶּה

ר. וְאָהַבְתָּ אֵת יְיָ אֱלֹהֶיךָ

ל. וְהָיוּ לְטֹטָפֹת בֵּין עֵינֶיךָ

ק. וּקְשַׁרְתָּם לְאוֹת עַל-יָדֶךָ

ה. וּבְלֶכְתְּךָ בַדֶּרֶךְ וּבְשָׁכְבְּךָ וּבְקוּמֶךָ

ע. אֲשֶׁר אָנֹכִי מְצַוְּךָ הַיּוֹם עַל-לְבָבֶךָ

מ. בְּכָל-לְבָבְךָ וּבְכָל-נַפְשְׁךָ וּבְכָל-מְאֹדֶךָ

> The suffix ךָ is one way of saying "your."

Find the phrase above that contains each of the following items. Write the letter of the phrase on the line.

1. Your house _____
2. Your God _____
3. Your hand _____
4. Your gates _____
5. A form of the Key Word, "love" _____
6. A form of the word מִצְוָה _____
7. More than one מְזוּזָה _____

According to the Torah, the שְׁמַע and וְאָהַבְתָּ should be recited twice each day.
From your answers, fill in the letters for each clue to discover when they are said.

```
5    3    4    7         1    2    6
                .
____ ____ ____ ____    ____ ____ ____
    ּ         ָ            ּ    ּ
```

וְאָהַבְתָּ

The שְׁמַע and וְאָהַבְתָּ are important parts of the service in all synagogues. In Traditional congregations, וְאָהַבְתָּ is followed by two other paragraphs. In Liberal congregations, only וְאָהַבְתָּ and part of the third paragraph are recited.

Practice reading the וְאָהַבְתָּ with a partner.

You shall love Adonai your God	1. וְאָהַבְתָּ אֵת יְיָ אֱלֹהֶיךָ
With all your heart, with all your life,	2. בְּכָל־לְבָבְךָ וּבְכָל־נַפְשְׁךָ
and with all your possessions.	3. וּבְכָל־מְאֹדֶךָ.
And these words	4. וְהָיוּ הַדְּבָרִים הָאֵלֶּה
which I command you this day	5. אֲשֶׁר אָנֹכִי מְצַוְּךָ הַיּוֹם
shall be upon your heart.	6. עַל־לְבָבֶךָ.
You shall teach them by heart to your children	7. וְשִׁנַּנְתָּם לְבָנֶיךָ
and speak of them when you sit in your house,	8. וְדִבַּרְתָּ בָּם בְּשִׁבְתְּךָ בְּבֵיתֶךָ
when you walk along the way,	9. וּבְלֶכְתְּךָ בַדֶּרֶךְ
when you lie down and when you rise up.	10. וּבְשָׁכְבְּךָ וּבְקוּמֶךָ.
Bind them as a sign upon your hand	11. וּקְשַׁרְתָּם לְאוֹת עַל־יָדֶךָ
and let them be a symbol between your eyes.	12. וְהָיוּ לְטֹטָפֹת בֵּין עֵינֶיךָ.
Write them on the doorposts of your house	13. וּכְתַבְתָּם עַל־מְזֻזוֹת בֵּיתֶךָ
and on your gates.	14. וּבִשְׁעָרֶיךָ.

This paragraph is one of the most poetic passages in the Bible. It tells us to live a life filled with holiness. It shows how our most common day-to-day activities become opportunities to show our love for God. Ordinary objects become symbols to remind us that living a Jewish life is important.

house = how we live

hand = what we do

head = what we _____

heart = what we _____

"YOUR house," "YOUR hand," "YOUR heart."
Now take a look at how Hebrew describes what we own.

Yours, Mine, and Yours

My or Mine	= שֶׁלִּי	= ■ יִ	+ שֶׁל
Yours (masc. sing.)	= שֶׁלְךָ	= ■ ךָ	+ שֶׁל
Yours (fem. sing.)	= שֶׁלָךְ	= ■ ךְ	+ שֶׁל

KEY WORD:
אַהֲבָה

Fill in the blanks with שֶׁלִּי, שֶׁלְךָ, or שֶׁלָךְ to make each sentence match its picture.

הַכֶּלֶב _____ ◆

הַחֲתוּלָה _____ ◆

הָאִמָּא _____ ◆

הַסֵּפֶר _____ ◆

הַבַּיִת _____ ◆

הַמִּשְׁפָּחָה _____ ◆

הַכִּתָּה _____ ◆

יוֹם-הֻלֶּדֶת _____ ◆

Language Enrichment

אוֹצַר מִלִים
A TREASURY OF WORDS

דֶּרֶךְ

between = בֵּין

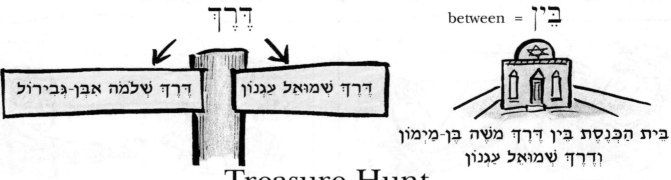

דֶּרֶךְ שְׁלֹמֹה אִבְּן-גְּבִירוֹל

דֶּרֶךְ שְׁמוּאֵל עַגְנוֹן

בֵּית הַכְּנֶסֶת בֵּין דֶּרֶךְ מֹשֶׁה בֶּן-מַיְמוֹן
וְדֶרֶךְ שְׁמוּאֵל עַגְנוֹן

Treasure Hunt

The path to the love of God is spelled out in the Jewish people's greatest treasure. Study the map on the next page and answer the questions below. Then unscramble the circled letters to find the treasure.

1. הַכֶּלֶב שֶׁל מִיכָאֵל עַל-יַד הַ◯_ _ _ שֶׁל יוֹסִי.

2. הַבַּיִת שֶׁל מִיכָאֵל עַל-יַד הַבַּיִת שֶׁל _ _ _◯_ .

3. הַמּוֹרָה בְּבֵית הַסֵּפֶר. בֵּית הַסֵּפֶר בְּדֶרֶךְ בֶּן-_ _ _ _ _◯ .

4. הַ_ _ _◯_ _ _ בְּדֶרֶךְ שְׁלֹמֹה אִבְּן-גְּבִירוֹל.

5. הַחֲתוּלָה שֶׁל רִבְקָה בָּעֵץ. הָעֵץ עַל-יַד הַבַּיִת שֶׁל _ _ _◯_ .

6. הָרַבִּי בְּבֵית הַכְּנֶסֶת. בֵּית הַכְּנֶסֶת בְּדֶרֶךְ מֹשֶׁה בֶּן-_ _ _◯_ .

7. הַבַּיִת שֶׁל רִבְקָה בְּדֶרֶךְ בֶּן-יְהוּדָה בֵּין דֶּרֶךְ רָשִׁי וְ_ _◯_ שְׁמוּאֵל עַגְנוֹן.

Unscramble the circled letters to find the treasure.

Where can we find the best ways to show our love for God?

_____ ___ _____   _____ ___ ___
ָ   ֲ   ֵ

***Now that you know where to look for the best ways of showing your love for God,
turn the page to find the most important way.***

Treasure Hunt Map

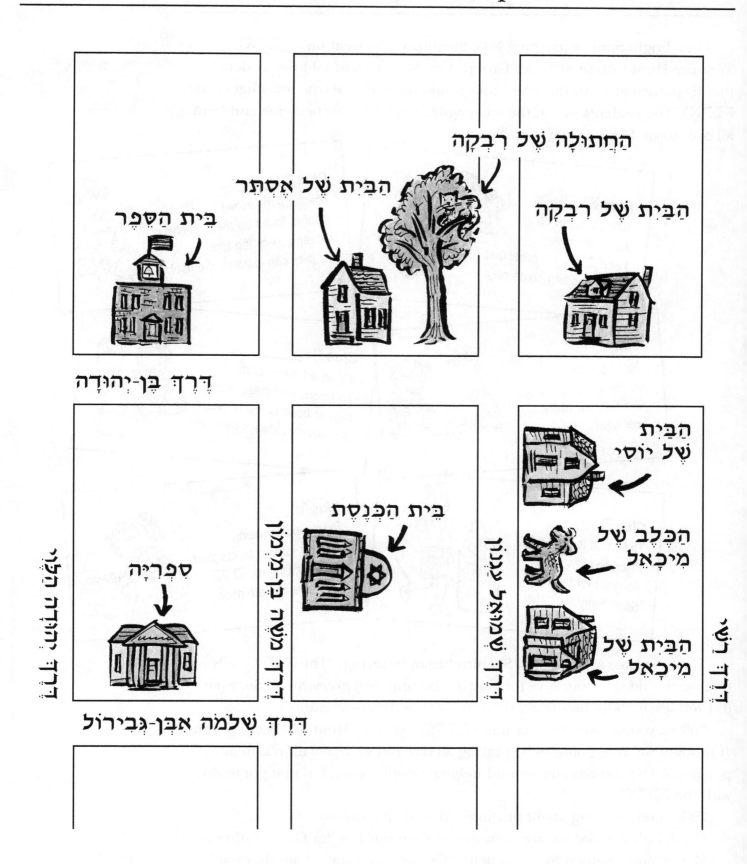

הַחֲתוּלָה שֶׁל רִבְקָה

הַבַּיִת שֶׁל אֶסְתֵּר

הַבַּיִת שֶׁל רִבְקָה

בֵּית הַסֵּפֶר

דֶּרֶךְ בֶּן-יְהוּדָה

הַבַּיִת שֶׁל יוֹסִי

הַכֶּלֶב שֶׁל מִיכָאֵל

הַבַּיִת שֶׁל מִיכָאֵל

בֵּית הַכְּנֶסֶת

סִפְרִיָּה

דֶּרֶךְ שְׁלֹמֹה אִבְּן-גְּבִירוֹל

The וְאָהַבְתָּ Treasure Hunt

On a bright Sunday morning Mrs. Shapiro's class went on a וְאָהַבְתָּ Treasure Hunt with their Youth Group. Mrs. Shapiro had told the students that by participating in this event they would discover the true meaning of the וְאָהַבְתָּ. The students met at the synagogue, received their first clue and went all over town. Here is what they did:

Clue א: _____
When you get up
And I am away
Feed כֶּלֶב his breakfast,
Then give him some play.

Clue ב: _____
Teach them to love
What is found on these shelves,
Or send them the tools
So they can learn by themselves.

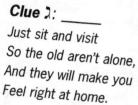

Clue ג: _____
Just sit and visit
So the old aren't alone,
And they will make you
Feel right at home.

Clue ד: _____
It's an art and a craft
To inscribe all these words
In your head and your heart
So they can always be heard.

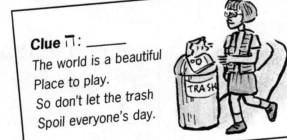

Clue ה: _____
The world is a beautiful
Place to play.
So don't let the trash
Spoil everyone's day.

Clue ו: _____
Thank you for being
Such honorable Mentschen
And for giving my כֶּלֶב
Some evening attention.

The next class session, Mrs. Shapiro began by saying, "The וְאָהַבְתָּ tells us that we should show our love for God all the time and everywhere. So, what did you learn about how to do this during your Treasure Hunt?"

"When you said we were having a וְאָהַבְתָּ Treasure Hunt," Rebecca began, "I thought we were going to be praying all day. But we really didn't do *any* praying. All we did was run around helping people. What has that got to do with the וְאָהַבְתָּ?"

"Who said anything about praying?" Mrs. Shapiro asked.

"Well, isn't that the way we're supposed show our love for God?" Esther asked.

Mrs. Shapiro paused for a moment. "Can anyone think of another way?"

"By putting up a מְזוּזָה!" Michael called out.

"Okay. Any other ideas?" Mrs. Shapiro looked around the room, but the rest of the class was silent. "I can see that this is not yet clear. Let's try something else. Do you remember the dream that Esther had when we were studying the אַהֲבַת עוֹלָם prayer?"

"I remember!" Yossi called out. "There were no rules!"

"Right. At the time we discussed the idea that God shows love for us by giving us rules. It's the same thing that parents do," Mrs. Shapiro added.

Danny spoke up. "Only God's rules are in the Torah."

Mrs. Shapiro nodded. "Exactly. The וְאָהַבְתָּ is also in the Torah, right after the Ten Commandments. So when the וְאָהַבְתָּ says, 'these words which I command you this day,' it's talking about the Ten Commandments, and really all of the מִצְוֹת."

"So, we're supposed to show our love back to God by doing מִצְוֹת?" Esther said. "I guess that makes sense."

"It really does if you think about it," Mrs. Shapiro agreed.

"Then why are we learning about prayer and the מְזוּזָה?" Sarah asked.

"Those are also important," Mrs. Shapiro answered, "because they remind us about what we're supposed to do."

"Like tying a string around your finger," Yossi said.

Isaac shook his head. "I tried that once. It didn't work because the string kept falling off!"

Mrs. Shapiro laughed. "The וְאָהַבְתָּ also mentions תְּפִלִּין. Putting on תְּפִלִּין is another special way to remember the importance of doing מִצְוֹת. It's like tying a leather 'string' around your fingers, arms, and head! I know that Yossi's dad puts on תְּפִלִּין. He could tell you all about how it helps him remember the מִצְוֹת."

"Yeah, Isaac," Yossi said. "If you ever need help tying a string around your finger, my Dad is a real expert!"

Complete the Treasure Hunt. Each of the Treasure Hunt clues on page 78 is related in some way to a phrase from the וְאָהַבְתָּ. Study the phrases, and write the number of the phrase on the clue that it best describes.

You shall teach them to your children	1. וְשִׁנַּנְתָּם לְבָנֶיךָ
and speak of them when you sit in your house,	2. וְדִבַּרְתָּ בָּם בְּשִׁבְתְּךָ בְּבֵיתֶךָ
when you walk along the way,	3. וּבְלֶכְתְּךָ בַדֶּרֶךְ
when you lie down	4. וּבְשָׁכְבְּךָ
and when you rise up	5. וּבְקוּמֶךָ
Write them on the doorposts of your house	6. וּכְתַבְתָּם עַל־מְזוּזוֹת בֵּיתֶךָ

On That Note

Life can be very short, and terrible tragedies can take away those we most love. For this reason, it is important to let our loved ones know how we feel about them whenever we can.

Write a short note to someone you really care about, describing how you feel (you don't have to actually send your note, but you can if you choose to). You can write to a friend, a family member, or even a pet.

_____

_____

_____

_____

_____

_____

Keep these loving thoughts and feelings in your heart as you recite the וְאָהַבְתָּ quietly to yourself.

וְאָהַבְתָּ אֵת יְיָ אֱלֹהֶיךָ בְּכָל-לְבָבְךָ וּבְכָל-נַפְשְׁךָ וּבְכָל-מְאֹדֶךָ.

וְהָיוּ הַדְּבָרִים הָאֵלֶּה אֲשֶׁר אָנֹכִי מְצַוְּךָ הַיּוֹם עַל-לְבָבֶךָ.

וְשִׁנַּנְתָּם לְבָנֶיךָ וְדִבַּרְתָּ בָּם בְּשִׁבְתְּךָ בְּבֵיתֶךָ וּבְלֶכְתְּךָ בַדֶּרֶךְ

וּבְשָׁכְבְּךָ וּבְקוּמֶךָ. וּקְשַׁרְתָּם לְאוֹת עַל-יָדֶךָ וְהָיוּ לְטֹטָפֹת

בֵּין עֵינֶיךָ. וּכְתַבְתָּם עַל-מְזֻזוֹת בֵּיתֶךָ וּבִשְׁעָרֶיךָ.

The Jewish philosopher Martin Buber wrote, "One who loves God brings God and the world together." The וְאָהַבְתָּ tells us how to show our love for God by bringing God into our daily lives.

Love can be a powerful force for good, but it can also be quite fragile. In order to be strong, love must be united with truth — אֱמֶת. When love and truth are bound together, miracles can happen, as you will see in Chapter 9.

CHAPTER 9

"Our God is the God of Truth"

KEY WORD:
אֱמֶת

Our tradition teaches that the Key Word, אֱמֶת, is the beginning, middle, and end of all things.

א ב ג ד ה ו ז ח ט י כ ך ל מ ם נ ן ס ע פ ף צ ץ ק ר ש ת

1. What is the first letter of the Hebrew alphabet? _____

   What letter is exactly in the middle? _____

   What is the last letter of the Hebrew alphabet? _____

2. What do these letters spell? _____

3. Explain why אֱמֶת is said to be the beginning, middle, and end of all things.

   _____

The שְׁמַע and מִי-כָמֹכָה are two passages from the Torah. In our service, אֱמֶת is the bridge between these two prayers. Study the excerpts from the evening אֱמֶת prayer. Then complete the activity to see how אֱמֶת creates a bridge.

אֱמֶת

שְׁמַע
Theme:
God is One.

This part of the אֱמֶת prayer has the theme of the שְׁמַע.

אֱמֶת וֶאֱמוּנָה כָּל-זֹאת
וְקַיָּם עָלֵינוּ כִּי הוּא יְיָ
אֱלֹהֵינוּ וְאֵין זוּלָתוֹ.

"True and faithful is all this, and required of us, for Adonai alone is our God; there is none else."

Circle the words from this passage that are related to the theme of the שְׁמַע.

This part of the אֱמֶת prayer has the theme of מִי-כָמֹכָה.

הַפּוֹדֵנוּ מִיַּד מְלָכִים
מַלְכֵּנוּ הַגּוֹאֲלֵנוּ
מִכַּף כָּל-הֶעָרִיצִים.

"God delivers us from the hands of oppressors, our Ruler, who saves us from the fists of tyrants."

מִי-כָמֹכָה
Theme:
_____
_____

Cross the אֱמֶת Bridge

With a partner, take turns reading these prayer phrases. Begin
with the שְׁמַע. If you make a mistake, you must begin again.
The first to read the מִי-כָמֹכָה correctly is the winner.

שְׁמַע יִשְׂרָאֵל יְיָ אֱלֹהֵינוּ, יְיָ אֶחָד.

אֱמֶת וֶאֱמוּנָה כָּל-זֹאת
וְקַיָּם עָלֵינוּ
כִּי הוּא יְיָ אֱלֹהֵינוּ
וְאֵין זוּלָתוֹ
וַאֲנַחְנוּ יִשְׂרָאֵל עַמּוֹ.
אֱמֶת וְיַצִּיב וְאָהוּב וְחָבִיב
וְנוֹרָא וְאַדִּיר וְטוֹב וְיָפֶה
הַדָּבָר הַזֶּה
עָלֵינוּ לְעוֹלָם וָעֶד.
אֱמֶת אֱלֹהֵי עוֹלָם
מַלְכֵּנוּ צוּר יַעֲקֹב
מָגֵן יִשְׁעֵנוּ.
הַפּוֹדֵנוּ מִיַּד מְלָכִים
מַלְכֵּנוּ הַגּוֹאֲלֵנוּ
מִכַּף כָּל-הֶעָרִיצִים.

מִי-כָמֹכָה בָּאֵלִם יְיָ?
מִי כָּמֹכָה נֶאְדָּר בַּקֹּדֶשׁ?
נוֹרָא תְהִלֹּת עֹשֵׂה פֶלֶא.

The Power of אֱמֶת

How great is the power of אֱמֶת? According to one version of an old legend, it holds the power of life and death. At a time of great persecution, Rabbi Yehuda Loew and his students decided to create a Golem, a magical creature shaped like a person, but with immense strength, to protect the Jewish community of Prague.

The Rabbi and his students went out at midnight on the night of the new moon. They made their way to the river Moldau, and on its banks they shaped the Golem. They recited mystical incantations and secret prayers as they worked. When the Golem was formed, Rabbi Yehuda Loew wrote the word אמת on the Golem's forehead, and the Golem opened its eyes. Then, just as God had breathed the breath of life into Adam, Rabbi Loew breathed into the Golem's mouth, and the Golem came to life.

They dressed the Golem in a spare set of clothes, and sent it out every night to watch over the Jewish community. According to the legend, the Golem was such a good protector that the persecutions soon came to an end, and the Golem had nothing to do. The Golem became bored, and gradually began to sneak out on its own. Because it was not really human, the Golem did not understand right and wrong, and eventually became wild and destructive.

Rabbi Loew decided that he must put an end to his Golem. So on the night of a new moon, he and his students took the Golem into the attic of the synagogue. They laid the Golem down on a bed of old prayerbooks, and recited the same incantations they had said on the night the Golem was created, but this time they said them in reverse. When the prayers were completed, Rabbi Loew erased the א from the Golem's forehead, leaving מת, which is Hebrew for "dead." Rabbi Loew covered the dead Golem with a bunch of old tallitot, and he put a sign on the entrance to the attic forbidding anyone to enter.

According to the legend, the Golem is still there, waiting for the time that it is once again needed to protect the Jewish people.

**Write the correct Hebrew word
on each Golem's forehead.**

מִי-כָמֹכָה

Climb the Pyramid

The מִי-כָמֹכָה was first recited by the Children of Israel as they escaped from Egypt. Start in the lower right hand corner, and read the words in each row to a partner. If you make a mistake, you must begin again. Keep reading until both of you can "climb" the pyramid without making a mistake.

TEXT EXploration

The מִי-כָמֹכָה is a prayer that asks a rhetorical question. Study this passage with a partner, and fill in the blanks that follow to find an answer to this prayer's rhetorical question.

> **RHETORICAL QUESTION:**
> (noun) A question that is asked to emphasize a point, support a position, or introduce a topic, with no answer being expected.

Who is like You, among the gods, Adonai?	מִי-כָמֹכָה בָּאֵלִם יְיָ?
Who is like You, glorious in uniqueness?	מִי-כָמֹכָה נֶאְדָּר בַּקֹּדֶשׁ?
Awesome in praises, making wonderous miracles.	נוֹרָא תְהִלֹּת עֹשֵׂה פֶלֶא.

1. What question is asked in the first two lines? "_____ is _____ God?"

2. The very first prayer we studied actually answers this question.
   (You can find it on page 8). Complete the English translation.
   Then write its name in Hebrew on the blank line.

   There is _____ Like Our God = _____

Wonder of Wonders! = פֶּלֶא עַל כָּל פֶּלֶא

In Israel, energy is very expensive. Because ovens require a great deal of energy to run, some Israelis bake cakes and casseroles by using a special pot known as a "wonder pot." A "wonder pot" looks like an angel food cake pan with a lid. It sits over a gas burner and has a special base that directs the heat up through its hollow center, causing the contents of the pot to bake.

פְּלֶאפוֹן   סִיר פֶּלֶא

1. What is the meaning of the key word פֶּלֶא?

_____

2. _____ful (masculine) = נִפְלָא

   _____ful (feminine) = נִפְלָאָה

3. How do you think the פְּלֶאפוֹן got its name? _____

YIDBIT

Acronyms are words that are built up from small parts of other words. Sometimes companies are known by acronyms of their full names. For example:

National Biscuit Company = Nabisco

There are lots of Hebrew acronyms. Some famous people are known by acronyms of their full Hebrew names and titles. For example:

רַבִּי מֹשֶׁה בֶּן-מַיְמוֹן = רַמְבַּ"ם

רַבִּי שְׁלֹמֹה בֶּן יִצְחָק = רַשִׁ"י

It is possible that an acronym of the מִי-כָמֹכָה became the nickname for one of the most famous heroes in Jewish history. Nearly 2200 years ago, a foreign tyrant who ruled over the Land of Israel demanded that everyone worship idols. A small band of Jews began fighting to win back their independence. Eventually, their leader became known by an acronym of the מִי-כָמֹכָה. To find this famous leader's name, fill in the blanks with the first letter from each word of the prayer's opening line. One letter has been filled in for you.

מִי-כָמֹכָה בָּאֵלִם יְיָ?

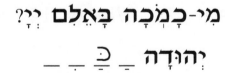

יְהוּדָה _ _ כַּ _ _

מִי־כָמְכָה

The מִי־כָמְכָה prayer is recited during both evening and morning services, but the lines that complete its blessing are different. In the evening, there is also a second blessing. It is called הַשְׁכִּיבֵנוּ. Study these versions of this prayer.

SHABBAT EVENING

Who is like you among the gods, Adonai?	1. מִי־כָמְכָה בָּאֵלִם יְיָ?
Who is like You, glorious in specialness?	2. מִי כָּמְכָה נֶאְדָּר בַּקֹּדֶשׁ?
Awesome in praises, making wonders.	3. נוֹרָא תְהִלֹּת עֹשֵׂה פֶלֶא.
Your children saw Your majesty when	4. מַלְכוּתְךָ רָאוּ בָנֶיךָ
You split the sea before Moses,	5. בּוֹקֵעַ יָם לִפְנֵי מֹשֶׁה
This is my God they responded and said:	6. זֶה אֵלִי עָנוּ וְאָמְרוּ:
The Eternal will reign forever and ever.	7. יְיָ יִמְלֹךְ לְעֹלָם וָעֶד.
And it is said that the Eternal redeemed Jacob,	8. וְנֶאֱמַר כִּי־פָדָה יְיָ אֶת יַעֲקֹב,
rescuing him from one stronger than himself.	9. וּגְאָלוֹ מִיַּד חָזָק מִמֶּנּוּ.
Blessed are You, Adonai, the Rescuer of Israel.	10. בָּרוּךְ אַתָּה יְיָ גָּאַל יִשְׂרָאֵל.

Lie us down, Adonai our God, in peace	1. הַשְׁכִּיבֵנוּ יְיָ אֱלֹהֵנוּ לְשָׁלוֹם
and raise us up, our Ruler, to life.	2. וְהַעֲמִידֵנוּ מַלְכֵּנוּ לְחַיִּים.
Spread the shelter of Your peace over us,	3. וּפְרוֹשׂ עָלֵינוּ סֻכַּת שְׁלוֹמֶךָ,
and guide us with Your good counsel.	4. וְתַקְּנֵנוּ בְּעֵצָה טוֹבָה מִלְּפָנֶיךָ.
Save us for the sake of Your name.	5. וְהוֹשִׁיעֵנוּ לְמַעַן שְׁמֶךָ.
Shield us and protect us from	6. וְהָגֵן בַּעֲדֵנוּ וְהָסֵר מֵעָלֵינוּ
hatred, plague, war, famine and sorrow.	7. אוֹיֵב דֶּבֶר וְחֶרֶב וְרָעָב וְיָגוֹן.
Keep adversity far away from us,	8. וְהָסֵר שָׂטָן מִלְּפָנֵינוּ וּמֵאַחֲרֵינוּ,
and shelter us in the shadow of Your wings.	9. וּבְצֵל כְּנָפֶיךָ תַּסְתִּירֵנוּ.
For You are our guardian and our protector,	10. כִּי אֵל שׁוֹמְרֵנוּ וּמַצִּילֵנוּ אָתָּה.
our gracious and compassionate Ruler.	11. כִּי אֵל מֶלֶךְ חַנּוּן וְרַחוּם אָתָּה.
Guard our coming and our going	12. וּשְׁמוֹר צֵאתֵנוּ וּבוֹאֵנוּ
for life and for peace	13. לְחַיִּים וּלְשָׁלוֹם
now and forever.	14. מֵעַתָּה וְעַד עוֹלָם.
Spread the shelter of Your peace over us.	15. וּפְרוֹשׂ עָלֵינוּ סֻכַּת שְׁלוֹמֶךָ.
Blessed are You, Adonai,	16. בָּרוּךְ אַתָּה יְיָ
Whose shelter of peace is spread over us,	17. הַפּוֹרֵשׂ סֻכַּת שָׁלוֹם עָלֵינוּ,
over all Your people Israel,	18. וְעַל־כָּל־עַמּוֹ יִשְׂרָאֵל,
and over Jerusalem.	19. וְעַל יְרוּשָׁלָיִם.

Who is like You, among the gods, Adonai?	מִי־כָמְכָה בָּאֵלִם יְיָ? .1
Who is like You, glorious in specialness?	מִי כָמְכָה נֶאְדָּר בַּקֹּדֶשׁ? .2
Awesome in praises, making wonders.	נוֹרָא תְהִלֹת עֹשֵׂה פֶלֶא. .3
Those rescued sang a new song to Your Name	שִׁירָה חֲדָשָׁה שִׁבְּחוּ גְאוּלִים לְשִׁמְךָ .4
on the shores of the sea.	עַל־שְׂפַת הַיָּם. .5
Together all of them gave thanks	יַחַד כֻּלָּם הוֹדוּ .6
and crowned You and said:	וְהִמְלִיכוּ וְאָמְרוּ: .7
The Eternal will reign forever and ever.	יְיָ יִמְלֹךְ לְעֹלָם וָעֶד. .8
O Rock of Israel, rise up in help of Israel.	צוּר יִשְׂרָאֵל קוּמָה בְּעֶזְרַת יִשְׂרָאֵל. .9
Redeem Your scattered people, Judah and Israel.	וּפְדֵה כִנְאֻמֶךָ יְהוּדָה וְיִשְׂרָאֵל. .10
Our Rescuer, Adonai of Hosts is Your name,	גֹּאֲלֵנוּ יְיָ צְבָאוֹת שְׁמוֹ .11
The Special One of Israel.	קְדוֹשׁ יִשְׂרָאֵל. .12
Blessed are You Adonai,	בָּרוּךְ אַתָּה יְיָ .13
the Rescuer of Israel.	גָּאַל יִשְׂרָאֵל. .14

The מִי־כָמְכָה was first recited when the Children of Israel escaped the Pharaoh's chariots. The Sea of Reeds miraculously split for them. What other things have you heard described as miracles?

_____

_____

Wonder of Wonders,
Miracle of Miracles

"Okay," Mrs. Shapiro said as the class finished their answers. "Who can tell me what the main idea of the מִי־כָמֹכָה prayer is?"

"God rescued them with a miracle!" Daniel called out. "Things looked really bad and then suddenly everything turned out great."

"No way!" Yossi called from across the room. "There's no such thing as a miracle. It's just something people made up. If miracles are real, how come we don't see any of them happening today?"

"Well, what do you think?" Mrs. Shapiro asked.

"My dad said that it was a miracle the Mets won the 1969 World Series," Isaac answered. "He said they were called the 'Miracle Mets.'"

Mrs. Shapiro smiled. "I've always thought of miracles a little differently. Then again, I'm not really a baseball fan."

"When my baby cousin was born last month," Sarah said, "my mom said that a new baby is a real miracle."

"My baby sister was no miracle," Esther added. "Not when she was born and not now either."

"That doesn't count anyway," Yossi said. "Babies are born all the time. There's nothing special about that."

"So, you believe that a miracle has to be something unusual or out of the ordinary?" Mrs. Shapiro asked.

"Well, doesn't it?" Michael continued. "The oil lasting for eight days at Chanukah and the sea splitting in half were like impossible things that happened anyway. Isn't that what a miracle is?"

"I heard something really neat about that," Esther added. "These two scientists figured out that a big wind storm could have caused the sea to split. They said the Sea of Reeds gets all these powerful winds in the spring. The wind can get strong enough to push the water up to the side like a wall. Then if it suddenly stops, the water pours back in just a couple of minutes. It really could have happened just like the Torah says. Science proves it."

"If it's science," Yossi countered, "it isn't a miracle."

"Sure it is," Rebecca said. "My grandpa says that everything is a miracle. The sun rises every morning and that's a miracle. There are all kinds of plants and animals, and each one is special. He says that all of life is a miracle, even science."

"Maybe the wind could split the sea," Daniel continued, "and the miracle was that it happened at the right time to save the Israelites, then stopped in time to drown the Egyptians. My uncle lives in Israel and he told me that during the Gulf War, all these missiles kept landing in Israel, but they hit vacant lots and empty buildings instead of schools or office buildings. He said that felt like a miracle."

Mrs. Shapiro nodded. "Maybe the problem is not that miracles don't happen today. Maybe they happen all the time and we just don't recognize them."

1. Do you believe in miracles? _____Yes _____No

2. What do you think is a miracle? _____

Now that you've come to your journey's end, take a minute to think about the מִי-כָמֹכָה.

According to our tradition, every Jewish soul was present at the Exodus from Egypt — even those who had not yet been born. That is why we reenact this event every year at the Seder.

Imagine that you have just crossed the Sea of Reeds with Moses, narrowly escaping the Pharaoh's chariots.

YOU ARE HERE!
↓

Keep these images and feelings in your heart as you recite the מִי-כָמֹכָה *aloud with your class.*

מִי-כָמֹכָה בָּאֵלִם יְיָ?
מִי כָּמֹכָה נֶאְדָּר בַּקֹּדֶשׁ?
נוֹרָא תְהִלֹּת עֹשֵׂה פֶלֶא.

There is a wonderful custom that comes from the great Yeshivot. When the students completed a tractate of Talmud, they would hold a special celebration, called a סִיּוּם. Today, classes in Israel celebrate the end of the school year with a מְסִבַּת סִיּוּם. Mrs. Shapiro's class is already having their מְסִבַּת סִיּוּם. Before you can have yours, you must complete Mrs. Shapiro's final test.

Mrs. Shapiro's Final Test

Fill in the missing word from the choices in the box.

שֻׁלְחָן	יִצְחָק _____ אֶת הַלּוּחַ.
לוֹמֵד	דָּנִי לֹא _____ בַּקֵּיץ.
רוֹאֶה	הַמּוֹרָה רוֹאָה _____ תַּלְמִידוֹת.
רוֹאָה	רִבְקָה _____ מוּסִיקָה.
שׁוֹמַעַת	הַפִּיצָה שֶׁל יוֹסִי עַל הַ_____.
כִּסֵּא	הַכֶּלֶב שֶׁל מִיכָאֵל תַּחַת הַ_____.
שָׁלוֹשׁ	הַמּוֹרָה לֹא _____ אֶת הַכֶּלֶב!

Study the picture above. Write יֵשׁ or אֵין in the blank to make each statement correct.

_____ חָתוּל תַּחַת הַשֻּׁלְחָן.	_____ תּוֹרָה עִם רִמּוֹנִים.
_____ תַּלְמִידִים בְּלִי סְפָרִים.	_____ חַלָּה בֵּין הַקּוֹלָה וְהַפִּיצָה.
_____ מוּסִיקָה בַּכִּתָּה הַיּוֹם.	_____ עִבְרִית עַל הַלּוּחַ.
_____ כֶּלֶב בֵּין רִבְקָה וְאֶסְתֵּר.	_____ סֵפֶר בַּיָּד שֶׁל הַמּוֹרָה.

Mrs. Shapiro's Photo Album

Help Mrs. Shapiro complete her album for the year.
Write the correct caption under each of the pictures.

מִיכָאֵל   רִבְקָה   דָּנִי   אֶסְתֵּר   יוֹסִי   שָׂרָה   יִצְחָק

CAPTIONS

דָּנִי שׁוֹמֵעַ אֶת הַשְּׁמַע.

אֶסְתֵּר לוֹמֶדֶת עִבְרִית עִם יִצְחָק.

הַסִּפְרִיָּה בְּדֶרֶךְ שְׁלֹמֹה אִבְּן-גְּבִירוֹל.

יוֹם הֻלֶּדֶת שֶׁל שָׂרָה בַּחֹרֶף.

פֶּסַח חַג הָאָבִיב.

סְתָיו בְּבֵית-הַסֵּפֶר.

שְׁתֵּי תַּלְמִידוֹת עַל-יַד הַנֵּרוֹת.

יוֹסִי, לֹא כָּל יוֹם פּוּרִים.

91   CHAPTER **10**

Key Word Search

Many of the Key Words you have studied this year are connected to ideas that people have about God. Match each Key Word from the list below to the sentence that best describes it. Then circle the words in the puzzle to find the Jewish People's most important idea about God.

God said, "Let there be light!"   הַשֵּׁם

God Rules the whole Universe.   הָעוֹלָם

God has many names.   הָעֶרֶב

Our God is the God of truth.   הָאוֹר

God creates the evening, and other times.   אַהֲבָה

God's gift to the Jewish people.   אֱמֶת

God loves us. We love God.   מִצְוֹת

God gives us rules.   תּוֹרָה

Find and circle these Key Words in the puzzle to discover the Jewish People's most important idea about God. Hint: hidden words may be horizontal, vertical, or diagonal.

ר	וֹ	אָ	הָ	ם	צָ	ה	בְ	הֲ	אַ	צָ	סַ	ם	אָ	צָ	הַ	שָׁ
דְ	שָׁ	ת	ז	הַ	לֹ	מָ	אַ	הָ	חָ	כָ	דְ	לָ	ס	שֶׁ	ל
מְ	הֹ	וֹ	טַ	חָ	רַ	בְ	צָ	עֲ	יָ	מֶ	סַ	אֱ	וֹ	ם	וֹ
אָ	תַ	רָ	רְ	גַ	ת	וֹ	וּ	רְ	וֹ	בְ	יָ	טַ	מֶ	שָׁ	ע
ם	מֶ	הַ	צָ	מַ	הַ	תַ	דְ	ת	בַ	ם	ל	שָׁ	תָ	אָ	הָ

The most important Jewish idea: God is _____

A Letter from Rebecca

Dear Aunt Audrey,

How are you? I am fine. My mom is making me write this letter to you.

Thank you for sending me the birthday present. The gold חי is really cool! I wear it all the time. I could read it and tell my mom and dad what it means because I learned all about that word in Hebrew School.

I had a really good time in Hebrew this year, but don't tell anybody because Hebrew school isn't supposed to be fun. My teacher was Mrs. Shapiro. She made everything interesting. We learned lots of Hebrew words and all about the prayers. We had great discussions about God and stuff. It's even fun to go to services when you know what's going on.

Like last summer when I visited Grandma and Grandpa Mizrachi, Grandpa took me to services with him at the Sephardic synagogue. The songs were different and some of the prayers were really long. But this year we learned all about why the prayers are different in other synagogues. I can't wait to visit Grandma and Grandpa this summer! I guess that's all I have to say.

Love, Rebecca

A Letter from Aunt Audrey

Dear Rebecca,

What a treat it was to get your letter. I'm so glad that you liked the חי. It is just like the one I wear. You may remember that I got mine from my grandmother, and it is something I've always treasured.

I'm glad to hear that you enjoyed Hebrew School so much this year — don't worry, your secret is safe with me! Things sure have changed since I was in Hebrew School. All we ever did was practice sounding out words in Hebrew. We never learned what any of them meant, and we certainly never learned about the ideas in the prayers. It's exciting that you are getting to do all of those things. Maybe you can explain it all to me.

I can't wait to see you this summer! That's all for now.

Love, Aunt Audrey

Dear Aunt Audrey,

I showed your letter to Mrs. Shapiro and she asked everyone in the class to write their answers to your question about why it is important to pray.

Love, Rebecca

I think it is important to pray because: _____

The most interesting thing I've learned this year is: _____

The Journey Nears Its End

Fill in the blank line at each prayer's station with the prayer's main idea. Draw a moon next to each prayer that is recited in the evening, and a sun next to each that is recited in the morning.

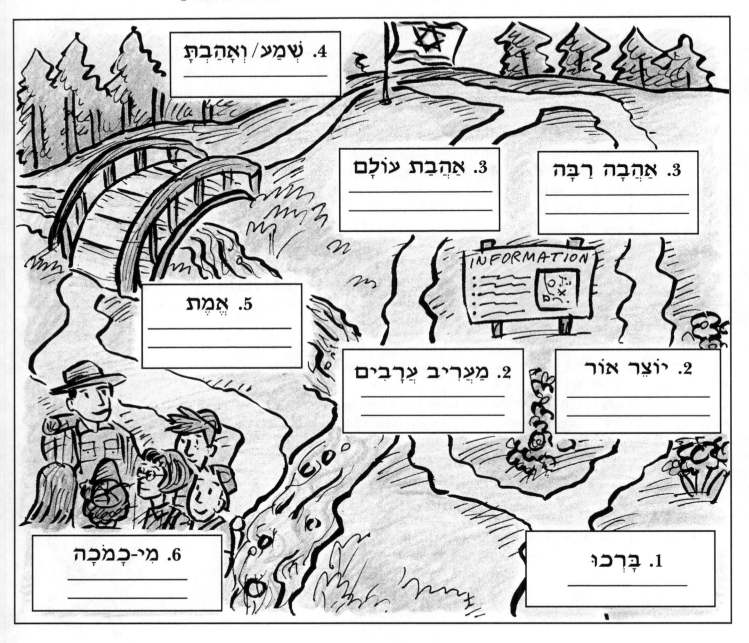

שְׁמַע/וְאָהַבְתָּ .4
_____

אַהֲבַת עוֹלָם .3
_____

אַהֲבָה רַבָּה .3
_____

אֱמֶת .5
_____

מַעֲרִיב עֲרָבִים .2
_____

יוֹצֵר אוֹר .2
_____

מִי־כָמֹכָה .6
_____

בָּרְכוּ .1
_____

You have reached the end of this "prayer journey"! You can now use your map to find your way through this part of the service at any time.

מַזָּל טוֹב!

Dictionary   מִלּוֹן

CHAPTER   **CHAPTER**

א

אָבִיב	(4) _____
אַבְנֵט	(5) _____
אַהֲבָה	(8) _____
אוֹר	(3) _____
אֶחָד	(7) _____
אַחַת	(7) _____
אֵין	(4) _____
אֱמֶת	(9) _____
אֲנִי	(1) _____
אֶפֶס	(7) _____
אַרְבַּע	(7) _____
אֵת	(1) _____
אַתָּה	(1) _____

ב

בֵּין	(8) _____
בְּלִי	(5) _____
בֹּקֶר	(3) _____

ד

דָּרוֹם	(2) _____
דֶּרֶךְ	(8) _____

ה

הוּא	(1) _____
הִיא	(1) _____

ח

חֹדֶשׁ	(4) _____
חָמֵשׁ	(7) _____
חֹרֶף	(4) _____
חֹשֶׁךְ	(3) _____
חֹשֶׁן	(5) _____

י

יוֹם	(3) _____
יוֹם הֻלֶּדֶת	(4) _____
יָרֵחַ	(3) _____
יֵשׁ	(4) _____

כ

כּוֹכָב	(3) _____
כַּמָּה	(7) _____
כֶּתֶר	(1) _____

ל

לוּחַ	(4) _____
לַיְלָה	(3) _____

מ

מְגִלָּה	(6) _____
מִזְרָח	(2) _____
מְלַמֵּד	(6) _____
מְלַמֶּדֶת	(6) _____
מִסְפַּר הַטֶּלֶפוֹן	(7) _____
מִסְפָּרִים	(7) _____
מְעִיל	(5) _____
מַעֲרָב	(2) _____
מִצְוָה	(5) _____
מָתַי	(4) _____

Dictionary מִלּוֹן

	CHAPTER	שׁ		CHAPTER	ס
_____	(7)	שֶׁבַע	_____	(6)	סוֹפֵר
_____	(6)	שׁוֹמֵעַ	_____	(6)	סִפּוּר
_____	(6)	שׁוֹמַעַת	_____	(6)	סִפְרִיָּה
_____	(1)	שֶׁל	_____	(6)	סַפְרָנִית
_____	(7)	שָׁלוֹשׁ	_____	(5)	סֵפֶר תּוֹרָה
_____	(1)	שֶׁלִּי	_____	(4)	סְתָיו
_____	(8)	שֶׁלְּךָ			ע
_____	(8)	שֶׁלֵּךְ	_____	(2)	עוֹלָם
_____	(1)	שֵׁם	_____	(5)	עִם
_____	(7)	שְׁמוֹנָה	_____	(5)	עֵץ חַיִּים
_____	(3)	שֶׁמֶשׁ	_____	(3)	עֶרֶב
_____	(3)	שַׁעַר	_____	(7)	עֶשֶׂר
_____	(7)	שֵׁשׁ			פ
_____	(7)	שְׁתַּיִם	_____	(10)	פֶּלֶא
_____	(7)	שְׁתֵּי			צ
		ת	_____	(2)	צָפוֹן
_____	(5)	תִּיק			ק
_____	(6)	תַּלְמוּד תּוֹרָה	_____	(4)	קַיִץ
_____	(7)	תֵּשַׁע			ר
			_____	(2)	רוֹאֶה
			_____	(2)	רוֹאָה
			_____	(5)	רִמּוֹנִים